To Hell in a Handcart

James Murphy

To Hell in a Handcart

© 2018 by James Murphy.

All rights reserved.

Published by The Heretic's Press
London
www.hereticspress.co.uk

By the same author

Poets (play-script)
The art of Exile (poetry)
The Misanthropist's Secret Love Life (poetry)
Lyrical Cynicism (poetry)
Disposophobia (play-script)
Crash the Bus (novel)
Handbook for the Damned (cultural & literary criticism)

ISBN 978-1-9996149-2-8
© 2018 The Heretic's Press
www.hereticspress.co.uk

Cover design by ZenXan Designs
zenxan@hotmail.com

To Hell in a Handcart

When love and logic collide…

A radical new play
about one summer in Nietzsche's life…

James Murphy

About The Author

Born in 1957, James Murphy grew up in the suburbs of South London. He graduated in Philosophy from the University of East Anglia at Norwich. He then worked in several different fields (sometimes literally), including journalism and teaching. During the 1980s, he lived in Tuscany. He now lives in Sussex, having recently fled over the border from Hampshire, where his house burned down (as per Nietzsche's Vesuvian exhortation). In addition to a novel, *Crash the Bus*, he has also written three further plays, *Poets* (about Byron & Shelley), *Stroke* and *Disposophobia*. He has also authored three collections of poetry: *The Misanthropist's Secret Love Life*, *The Art of Exile* and *Lyrical Cynicism*. A cultural and literary critique, *Handbook for the Damned* is currently going through the press. He is married with a son.

ABANDONED HOTEL

Why has the view changed? - It has not changed: the wooded hills, umbrella pines, the village bell tower, the single, dark-feathered, tropical pine, and the sea - blue leviathan! breathing in the curving bay. Still there.

For over a century, the hotel's scented clientele repeated their same languorous rituals in cream linen; drifted across the cool marble hall, ordered iced and sugared lemonade; took to the sweeping staircase, dismissed the porters, thronged the ornate balconies, let fall white parasols, lifted hats from heads, tilted pale faces to the sun and sky and chorused not-yet-jaded delight across the bay. And here and there, delicate flourishes of wrought iron still echo the fluted cadences of that long-forgotten tribe, and match, too, the languid curlicues of their cheque-books and bankers' drafts.

But now the balconies are unsafe. Here, only the trespasser's eye, trailing through the empty hotel rooms, gazes, as an afterthought, from the deserted shell, over the uncelebrated Italian hills.

Now, the view is simply life elsewhere, going on, unseen and un-admired, the telegraph wire sags above the scraggy pines, a stray dog sniffs corners, some scruffy local fishermen mend nets. Cheap housing creeps up the olive groves below the ruined monastery, and the hotel's unglazed windows stare out, blind and black, from the disintegrating walls.

Nietzsche, once the hotel's most renowned guest, wrote ecstatically in a letter to a friend: "There is something *Greek* about this place!"

But the old waiters recalled only a man who always pushed his food aside, and caught crumbs in his moustache...

Joanna Jones © 2013 The Heretic's Press

NIETZSCHE AS HUMAN DYNAMITE
(F. Nietzsche 1844-1900: a brief history of modern man as an explosive device)

When Nietzsche declared 'I am not a man, I am dynamite'[1], he employed the metaphor of himself as a human explosive device in a very precise as well as a poetic sense; since it is the job of dynamite to destroy. So it was that Nietzsche set the TNT of his philosophy around the foundations of a religio-ethical tradition he considered dangerously derelict – and stood back with an attendant sense of delight. In this context, Nietzsche is the most ironic of literary visionaries: an optimistic prophet of doom, he foresaw societal dissolution as a necessary precondition for cultural renewal. If Europe's great religious and ethical systems were moribund (as he saw it); let us be honest undertakers and commit them to the ashes; only then could the phoenix of a new culture be reborn. Certainly, in this philosophical stance Nietzsche affirms his own much-vaunted Dionysian principles, insofar as the Greek god delighted as he destroyed.

Not that the great philosopher was satisfied simply to destroy old, redundant values: in Nietzsche's view the new man, or 'Over-Man' (übermensch) would have to seize the fire and, Prometheus-like, restore vision to mankind through his own intellectual probity and (a)moral daring. This would involve a continuous 'self-overcoming' (selbstüberwindung) in which his vying drives and passions were continuously refined and reconciled. This heroic task would, Nietzsche proposed, replace the old, superseded spiritual or religious quest.

It is in this role as a major ethical, intellectual and psychological innovator that Nietzsche can be seen as Europe's last great classical polymath philosopher; i.e., one fixing his gaze on an all-round 360° view of man, taking in his ethics, aesthetics and religious instincts - in contrast to the 20th century's minor, post-structural (mainly Marxist) theorists with their dry, Cyclopean, uber-cerebral obsession with man's relationship to, and use of, language. Nietzsche's 'wicked thoughts'[2], however, are panoptic and as such largely responsible for the cultural upheaval in whose midst we still live today.

*1 Ecce Homo. *2 Beyond Good and Evil, (296)

1

And he desired no less. For Nietzsche saw himself as a messenger raising the alarm, a herald warning modern man about the dangerous new age that had dawned while he had lain sleeping, unleashing forces with which he would now either have to come to dramatic terms - or be destroyed.

With typical fin de siècle élan, Nietzsche declared that the Age of Enlightenment and the Industrial revolution had done far more than merely revolutionize man's way of life, they had radically restructured his very consciousness. As if overnight, science, reason and technology now explained the world and man's part in it. Darwin's evolutionism had proved our descent not from Adam and Eve but from apes. Thus, unwittingly, man had modernised himself out of any need for god and religion - and yet insodoing had ironically and tragically also robbed himself of all sense of meaning, since, as Nietzsche observed, man cannot live by facts alone – whether empirical or theoretical. On the contrary, his heart is driven by a desperate need for something transcendent to satisfy what Shakespeare described (in Anthony & Cleopatra) as man's "immortal longings," and to guide his ethical and aesthetic aspirations towards excellence. So where was this source of transcendent value now to be located? What could we realistically believe in to inspire us? Was this kind of belief even possible any more, now that all our time-honoured credos, myths, beliefs and convictions had – without us even realising it - become utterly obsolete and useless.

This cataclysm it was that Nietzsche had summed up in his infamous phrase 'God is dead' -

"God is dead... and we have killed him. How shall we comfort ourselves, the murderers of all murderers? What was holiest and mightiest of all that the world has yet owned has bled to death under our knives: who shall wipe this blood off us? ... Is not the greatness of this deed too great for us? Must we ourselves not become gods simply to appear worthy of it?" [3]

*3 Gay Science section 125

Indeed, modern man's fate was both ironically terrible and terribly ironic (as Nietzsche saw it), insofar as bourgeois, industrial, increasingly technological society had become not just unbearably meaningless, but also at the same time comfortably bearable. This savagely ambivalent experience is endured and enjoyed by Nietzsche's so-called 'Last Man,' a being suffocated by his own mediocre contentment, seething with saccharine discontent and thinly veiled neurosis (Freud was, of course, waiting just around the corner ready to wield his magnifying glass at said "last man's" unconscious). As such, man - and the society in which he lived - was a moral and spiritual catastrophe waiting to happen (and so, of course, it was to prove in the ensuing, almost hallucinogenically blood-stained 20th century).

In this context, then, Nietzsche's revelation of God's death was no vainglorious atheistic rant, but rather an epiphany, an annunciation of inverse biblical proportions to match that of the archangel Gabriel in his address to the Virgin Mary. For if God was, indeed, dead, then so, too, was all authority for moral absolutism of whatsoever kind.

The old order had entirely collapsed. In its place, as the dust cleared, stood the dangerous new pagan god of moral relativism, with his Nietzschean decree that the value and quality of an act could only now be judged *relative to the point of view* of the perpetrator or recipient of its effects (an interpretation also known as perspectivism). In the flash of a Nietzschean eye, morality could now be traced back to man's 'all-too-human' desires! His moral values were (as Nietzsche averred in 'Beyond Good and Evil,' no more than a confession of his personal appetite for certain truths and his capricious disgust for others.

On this basis Nietzsche unveiled his hugely controversial concept of 'master' and 'slave' morality (vis. On the Genealogy of Morals). In a nutshell, 'master morality' was the preserve of the few, the strong-willed, the noble-minded, the emotionally independent: those who imposed values by the sheer force of their personalities and talents. Conversely, 'slave morality' was imposed by those who, possessing none of the master's characteristics themselves, banded together to undermine and eventually outlaw them. (Strangely enough, the visionary poet William Blake, with whose fiery artistic temperament Nietzsche's own has, it seems to us, much in common, had himself observed a century earlier in 'The Marriage of Heaven and Hell: 'Those who restrain desire, do so because theirs is weak enough to be restrained.')

Of course, in heralding these new pagan moral gods, Nietzsche knew very well that he was setting the nihilistic cat amongst the moralistic pigeons (vis. 'Why I am so clever', Ecce Homo). Indeed, critics have blamed Nietzsche's philosophy, with its infamous reference to 'the blond beasts' (whose autocratic might was, by definition, right) for opening the door to predatory forces unredeemed by any concept or practice of pity - Nazi Germany being only the most obvious example. However, this is an over-simplification of Nietzsche's moral philosophy in gross political terms. For Nietzsche, 'spiritual aristocrats' would ultimately employ their master morality not principally on others, *but on themselves*. By constantly calling upon their own inner strengths to overcome the rigours and vicissitudes of fate they would achieve victory over it.

Thus Nietzsche famously focused his philosophy around the concept of 'the will to power,' not just because power was needed to effect real change, but because power was the animating principle of life itself! - the force of which man simultaneously partook and of which he was the highest imaginative expression. In short, life was power, and to triumph over its challenge man had to be powerful.

Nietzsche's objection to so much of the philosophical theory and inquiry throughout history was that it had ultimately been productive only of an escapism that had fled the stark reality of the human condition and insodoing fostered moral and spiritual weakness.

By the same criterion Nietzsche was skeptical of the new faith contemporary intellectuals were putting in modern science and scientific method. Conversely, and highly controversially, Nietzsche declared that so-called 'objective truth', however scientifically valid, was, in reality, no failsafe criterion of a fact's ultimate importance to mankind's development. To Nietzsche, a fact could be both true and harmful and - *whilst accepted on a rational level* – ought still, therefore, to be treated with extreme caution.

Darwin's theory of evolution was one such. Nietzsche accepted the broad sweep of the theory (with certain Nietzschean reservations*) but viewed its implications as potentially extraordinarily damaging. In the wrong hands he saw that Darwin's revelation would lead to a toxic nihilism, an absolute loss of faith in man as a creature capable of any extraordinary aspirations above those of survival, mutual exploitation and domination. Fatally, the fact that we now conceded we had descended from apes blocked any seriously tenable claim to an ethereal, aesthetic and spiritual view of man.

It was in this context, that Nietzsche warned of the need for a loftier view of the landscape that Darwin had revealed. We may well be 'risen apes', but - and contrary to the gloomy predictions of nihilism - what visions might this hominid creature now see in his upright state; what internal and external panoramas would open themselves to him: this 'risen angel' whose new 360° field of vision unified his understanding with new perspectives! - This utterly unique creature that could now look not only down and around, but up and beyond – not to mention backwards and forwards in time!

It was from this unique perspective, then, that Nietzsche regarded the new world of post-Enlightenment, post Darwinian scientific inquiry. Far from uncritically admiring its claim to access a new kind of absolute 'truth', he warned that 'positivism' was itself hardening into a new kind of dogma, one that threatened to damage man – precisely by limiting his view of himself to such mechanistic methods and concerns! Conversely (and to reiterate), a scientific fact or philosophical value was desirable if - and only if - it accessed man's crucial will-to-power (i.e., inspired him 'body and soul' [to use an un-Nietzschean phrase!]) and thereby drove him towards the fulfillment of his talents and potential. Again, in this context logic and reason were not in themselves ideals to be striven for, but rather tools to be taken up (or put down) appropriately at the right time and place in man's 'spiritual' quest. Alongside such tools existed others such as imagination, fantasy and what might (very) loosely be termed 'the religious urge', which still had a major part to play in man's development. Indeed, the past proved that even certain fruitful types of 'error' had a function and could prove useful if they challenged man to transcend himself - our earlier belief in 'God' being perhaps the prime example.

However, given that we cannot any longer, in all modern intellectual honesty, believe in god, then in whom or what are we are to repose our ideal of an awe-inspiring ideal? Where is the locus of the sacred for us, the repository of our treasured beliefs and convictions? What manifests our sense of, and capacity for, worship? For though god may be dead, mankind does seem to need to worship, does seem to need to be fed and nourished by a sense of 'something far more deeply interfused' (as Wordsworth had put it fifty years earlier) above and beyond, that is, a merely materialistic and mechanical view of the universe espoused by modern science.

Above all, these were not, it must be stressed, merely academic questions; on the contrary the answers we provided would shape the course of the next phase of human evolution. As Nietzsche saw it, there would be serious conflict between those who sought dangerous answers ('we aeronauts of the spirit') and those ('herd members') who preferred the terra firma of various forms of political, scientific and religious orthodoxy.

Of course, with typically Nietzschean irony, the philosopher embraced such a conflict, he saw it as a force for the 'good' insofar as it catalyzed man's deeper conscience, accessing the dynamic of change and the possibility for spiritual renewal.

Indeed, Nietzsche's vision of humanity was an essentially dynamic one. He believed man accessed this will-to-power and achieved moral, psychological, aesthetic and spiritual excellence only by tapping into the enormous forces of the psyche. This was to be done not by taming man's energies but by releasing them; not by binding him up in the kind of moralising, politically-correct red tape that would become so beloved of the various totalitarianisms of the 20th century (including our own deceptively mild-mannered social democratic version), but by freeing up the individual's flair for excellence using whatever means possible.

Similarly, deep thought and feeling - great art itself - came not from eradicating conflict but by promoting it, by the clash of psychophysical forces in the arena of the soul! Paramount was the awakening of man's energies and their sublimation for use in the quest for spiritual and cultural excellence. It was in such a context that Nietzsche had originally - and controversially - developed his theme (in 'The Birth of Tragedy, out of the Spirit of Music') that ancient Greece had achieved philosophical and aesthetic excellence not in spite of the age's constant violence, but because of it! – i.e., by accessing turbulent energy, then channeling it and sublimating it in the service of a higher (aesthetic) impulse.

My own belief is that, insofar as it guides the individual towards some, admittedly vague but nevertheless ultimate state of (super)consciousness, Nietzsche's 'self-overcoming' is itself 'absolutist' in nature, insofar as it represents one single, over-arching principle dominant in the heart and mind of the 'superman'. Similarly (and also ironically), I would suggest that Nietzsche embraced relativism only in a 'relative' sense, to help free man's mind of the chains imposed by Christianity's coarse theistic absolutism. Vitally, (I conjecture) Nietzsche would not have resorted to relativism as a moral get-out-of-jail-free card for casual every day use; i.e., to enable man to avoid all ethical responsibility simply by declaring "I do as I like' or by deflecting blame for his own manifest failings onto his own cultural circumstances. On the contrary, Nietzsche would have viewed such a version of relativism as a manifestation of weak 'slave morality' (as aforementioned); i.e., one which ultimately buttressed man's transparent inner weakness with the outward trappings of a false grandeur.

On the contrary, Nietzsche saw life as a crucial dialectical challenge that had to be faced in order to bring about a new synthesis in the soul. Partaking of both the physical and the mental world, man should embrace the spiritual turbulence, the host of warring opposites inside him: the poles of chaos versus form, nature versus reason, Apollo versus Dionysus, gods versus goddesses, men versus women, love versus hate, solitude versus company, etc – and imaginatively procreate from the struggle a dynamic new, transcendent form of himself.

Thus it was precisely in order not just to endure but to profit from such oppositional dynamics Nietzsche encouraged the practice of psychological and emotional self-reliance. Not, we hasten to add, in the sense of a banal, mechanical alienation from one's fellow men and women as a means of self-protection, but rather as a capacity boldly to enter the fires of experience and be refined by them; again, not to cast blame for *what* one experiences, but to accept it as a necessary conclusion of who one is as a human being.

Unsurprisingly, in this connection, Nietzsche was profoundly opposed to what post-war psychology would refer to as 'Group-think', of whichever persuasion – be it religious or secular, communist or capitalist. Like most authentic individuals, he loathed the insincere spirit of impotent concord. Indeed, for Nietzsche, an inner and outer spiritual war was vital if the individual was to repel the intense pressure for conformity exerted on him by post-industrial mass society. The question confronting us, as Nietzsche saw it, was – and is - are we, as individuals, prepared to undertake such a challenge, to subject ourselves to the artistic, ethical and spiritual training which Nietzsche recommends? (Interesting to remind ourselves here that Aristotle's philosophy students co-existed with their counterparts in physical competition at a training ground [gymnasium] known as the Lyceum.)

However, timeless though his philosophy is, and ultra-modern though he was for his era, as Nietzsche approached that fateful summer of 1882 he still lived in what we regard as an antiquated sociopolitical environment. The loose collections of German and Italian states had achieved their respective unifications only a decade or so earlier. Furthermore, the incipient democracies whose influence for mediocrity Nietzsche deplored, did not, in excluding women, extend to even half the populations of Europe; far less, in fact, inasmuch as property qualifications also ruled out vast swathes of less well-off men too.

Culturally, too, Nietzsche still lived in an ostensibly classical aesthetic age, a time when poetic and painterly abstractionism were, for instance, in their earliest infancy; when technology in the shape of the rudimentary camera and even more basic gramophone had only just begun to reach out and touch the arts; an age in which cinema was an as yet distant dream. Thus, though Nietzsche prophesied much about the 'shape of things to come', we are entitled to ask: was he right? Indeed, it is we, Nietzsche's descendants, who are the living test and proof of his prophecies. As such, we have the luxury of comparing his foresight with our own hindsight. With this perspective it is clear that Nietzsche was largely correct about our fate as 'moderns' in the West.

Though, in happier moments we like to think we have 'progressed' as a species – certainly we no longer execute children for poaching, or dump our 'criminals' in Australia. Still, in our digital, post-modern, post-religious, 'post-everything' age, a voice of doubt whispers to us from deep within the 'white noise' of modern collective conscience. We can't dispel the sense that somehow, over the past couple of centuries, we have suffered a catastrophic crisis of spiritual conscience, of value and meaning. In this respect we concede we are in deep trouble: yes, God is dead, and we wouldn't (it appears) have it any other way, but surrounded by material luxury as we are in the West, something crucial is missing. Try as we might we can't avoid returning again and again to the conclusion that we live spiritually impoverished lives. No doubt this stark predicament is neither easy to bear nor to resolve, and hence our resort to hedonic denial.

However, perhaps we should be patient. New cultures take time to evolve.

At a growing distance of many decades from the great world wars, and after several false starts, only now, perhaps, have we gained sufficient perspective to ask what kind of 'brave new world' we are remaking for ourselves. Certainly, as Nietzsche predicted, over the past century much cultural re-building has taken place and structures of dubious purpose and design have risen metaphorically and actually into the skies of our capitals once again. But will they last? *Should they?*

In this respect, the actual and philosophical collapse of both Communism's Berlin Wall and Capitalism's Twin Towers in New York on 9/11 have become iconic symbols of modern existentialist doubt and anxiety. All that is now certain is that the psychological architecture of our age teeters dangerously in the balance; not unlike one of those precariously swaying Japanese skyscrapers brilliantly engineered to withstand earthquakes. What, incidentally, is the primary effect of war if not a cultural earthquake in which the ground of traditional belief splits beneath our feet? Additionally, it is a distinct irony that when war ends, the declaration of peace merely marks the opening of philosophical hostilities, the vicious war of ideas about what shape that peace should take. As a result (and as Auden pre-eminently observed in his poem 'Age of Anxiety'), an intense sense of social and personal fragility has become the keynote experience of the age, itself inducing a kind of paralysis of the will, with the individual caught in trepidation between hostile ideologies. In a nutshell: if religion is passé, and modern democracy impotent; if the materialistic, nationalistic and imperialistic values that caused the great internecine wars of the 20th century are self-evidently dysfunctional, what shall we replace them with?

Of course, human nature being what it is, there has been no shortage of easy answers. From the soap-box arena of the world's parliaments and senate houses we hear politicians pompously speechifying about 'getting back to basics'; whilst from the other corner, various soi-disant Modernist, New-Age practitioners berate us vaingloriously about the need for a radical 'year zero' re-evaluation of those self-same traditional values. Indeed, such is our understandable confusion that much of the time we find ourselves agreeing and disagreeing with both simultaneously. It is surely no coincidence that our age has come up with the phrase 'cognitive dissonance' to describe just such an experience. Certainly, as a celebrant of intellectual conflict, Nietzsche, we venture to suggest, would have clapped his hands with glee at the bizarrely ambiguous sight and sound of us – and then shed a tear....

To a large extent our very capacity to question our own mediocrity is a problem. No doubt if we could, as a species, eradicate the vicious three-lettered word 'why' from our vocabulary, everything would be a lot simpler. Fortunately we can't. Like it or not - and enjoyable as the realm of the senses is – sensual gratification can never satisfy us for long. The search for exalted meaning and value constitutes the quintessence of human nature. Ultimately, such is the mysterious divinity of our nature, we cannot live full lives without a sense of transcendent purpose. So what is it that engenders it?

Nietzsche was plain in his answer to this question: Art, with a capital 'A'. As he famously declared: 'Only as an aesthetic phenomenon is existence and the world bearable' as he declared in an early work 'The Birth of Tragedy (Out of the Spirit of Music).'

Conversely, bereft of art, life was merely bestial, animalistic, a barely-refined hunt for sensual gratification.

But, of course, and as aforementioned, art has changed drastically since Nietzsche's day. Its aims and ambitions have mutated; so, too, the forms by which these are communicated. Yet, though its media may change, great art's timeless purpose to communicate eternal truths in contemporary language remains immutable (pace post-modernism – however the latter phenomenon may or may not be defined!).

Indeed, in this respect one might argue that, artistically-speaking, every age gets the master-medium its temperament deserves. The Elizabethans, for example (in chauvinistic Anglophone terms), had drama; the Romantics, poetry. Could it not be, then, that, for us, the camera, with its motor-driven shutter speed, is now the quick-fire soul of our blink-of-an-eye age; the photographic image its stunned conscience? There has been much, indeed, for it to capture.

Following a catastrophic 20th century of conflict and ideological savagery, arguably the most enduring image of our age is the devastated cityscape; Hiroshima, Nagasaki, the great capitals of Europe reduced to rubble, vast buildings fragmented, great walls collapsed; refugees filing faithlessly out of the ruined, smoking capitals of East and West towards the fragile safe house of modernism.

But where is it?

No doubt we are still in the process of finding out. In this sense, and though we do not realize it, we are mythically akin to Cadmus sowing the dragon's teeth on Theban soil in an effort to establish a firm footing in fate's uncertain landscape. Cadmus was brave, indomitable, solitary when necessary, loving in company. Above all, he knew how to remain faithful to an ideal. In possessing these qualities, and whilst mythical, it is vital to remember that Cadmus is not a myth, but an archetype of us, our human-ness, and as such his powers lie within each one of us. This is also true of Nietzsche, a lover of Greek mythology, who has, himself, in a very real way, begun to become a modern myth, a human we can emulate, each according to his or her talents. Indeed, his works are mysterious guidebooks that teach us how to prosecute our own talents, reverence our strengths and exorcise our weaknesses.

In this context, for his searingly honest indictment of our state and his fearless advocacy of what might be called the new humanist adventure, Nietzsche stands as a colossus astride our cultural abyss.

Indeed, if modernism is to establish a truly inspiring and lasting tradition, then, architecturally-speaking, Nietzsche, with his radical views on morality, art, religion and politics, is one of the main gates through which one must enter its cultural citadel; some would argue he is the great gate under whose arch we must pass if we want to get to – and at - the heart of the contemporary cultural experience. For with his sunlit energy and dynamic intellect Nietzsche is an antidote to our diseased age of anxiety and loss of cultural confidence masquerading as pseudo-egalitarianism. His medicine consists in a healthy recourse to spiritual rigour and honesty, a world without excuses, blame and a general deflection of responsibility onto third party circumstances. As such, he stands up for the individual in a way that his spiritual precursor William Blake would have loved. Doubtless, these two titans would have warred intellectually, but they would surely have loved each other's philosophical élan and vision. Indeed, one can almost hear Nietzsche across the centuries applauding and perhaps even accompanying on the piano(!) Blake's great song and call-to-spiritual-arms in his beautiful poem - incantation is a better word - Jerusalem:

'Bring me my Bow of burning gold; Bring me my Arrows of desire:
Bring me my Spear: O clouds unfold! Bring me my Chariot of fire!

Great souls pass on transcendent ideals to successive generations - without them vision founders. In our age, beset as it is by essentially inhuman materialistic and corporate forces seeking to eclipse man's hunger and capacity for that same sublime excellence, Nietzsche's crucial message has never been more relevant.

James Murphy. East Harting, The South Downs, West Sussex. Summer-Autumn 2018.

TO HELL IN A HANDCART

Author's Preface

Nietzsche delights in delivering crazy insights; perceptions at times so manifestly counterintuitive you feel he's making fun of the reader, as if saying 'I dare you to follow me here - dare you to believe me!' And frequently you do follow (such is the poetic charm of his style and his reasoning), only too late to turn round and see Nietzsche has led you up to and over the edge of an intellectual precipice, so that you feel your legs suddenly treading thin air above an abyss, like a cartoon character about to plunge to his doom. That's when you hear the great philosopher laughing. Indeed, that's the whole purpose of reading Nietzsche: to have the comfortable, existential rug pulled out from under your feet, to fall (as it were) through your own beliefs and realise they were nothing more than a thin veneer placed over a gaping hole, itself leading down to a much older, weirder substrate.

Indeed, Nietzsche wants us to realise that everything we think, feel and believe has sources and origins that are much deeper, older and more mysterious than we like to believe.

But that leads us to another problem: Nietzsche is so full of paradoxes we sometimes don't know which way to turn, which intellectual direction to face. Indeed, just *who* was Nietzsche; who is he today? Is he the voluntary spiritual outcast who longed for establishment recognition; the loner who loved people, the misogynist who loved women? (In reality, during the course of his relatively brief authorial life Nietzsche had two or three women friends whom he deeply respected.) The question remains: is there a discernible personality, specific identity behind the paradoxes? If not, how can one possibly attempt to represent Nietzsche dramatically?

Indeed, given both his titanic status in the temple of Western literature and the protean, complex nature of the man himself, to write a play about Nietzsche - indeed, to put words in Nietzsche's mouth - must itself surely rate as an act of aesthetic hubris of reckless proportions - how dare one assert one's suitability for such a task? The short answer is sheer Nietzschean effrontery; indeed, a poetic insolence for accepted values of literary humility the like of which we would fain think Nietzsche himself might have applauded!

That said, in a certain sheepish sense (that is, with mock humility aforethought) where *To Hell in a Handcart* is concerned, one almost had no say in the matter. In the middle of 2013's long hot summer, sudden encouragement by circumstance, and two or three beloved individuals who ought to have known better, conspired with one's own healthy egotism to seat one over the unforgiving keyboard to tap out the first exchanges of a drama one had always presumed was destined to remain nothing more than a pleasant literary daydream. Of course, once begun, it was too late....

To the extent that one writes about the people and psychological types who fascinate one, I number myself in the cohorts of moderns who have loved Nietzsche. Whilst allowing myself the luxury of disagreeing with some of his conclusions, like all great cultural innovators, Nietzsche preys on one's mind; he is a plague on one's conscience; once read, he does not leave you alone. Indeed, to pick up one of Nietzsche's books is to be conscious of the spiritual dynamite in one's hands. The question then follows: to what use will one put this spiritual explosive in one's own life?

In this regard, artists respond to each other almost involuntarily. Moreover, if one is inspired by the life and work of one's fellow men and women one has no choice but to absorb the spirit of their works - indeed, one opens wide one's arms to embrace their influence. This may or may not lead to the critic Harold Bloom's famous 'anxiety', as each new generation of poets struggles to avoid mere idolatrous replication, and insodoing find its own voice; but the fact remains that the spirit of emulation is essential to the cultural evolution of our species. We need heroes and heroines to prove to us that heroic acts of feeling, thought and action are indeed possible and realisable.

Ironically, Nietzsche himself was distinctly suspicious of the spirit of emulation. No doubt he saw much in it that was actually an unconscious subservience masquerading as aspiration. In this context he was famously averse to the adoption of a rigid (and therefore, in his opinion, false) code of emulation in something like Kempis's 'Imitation of Christ.' which he contemned as an emotionally enfeebling act of conformity. However, it will not be sensibly denied that the whole actual and spiritual thrust of the artist is to inspire in the audience the very values and experience contained in, and communicated by, the work of art.

In this way – and to put it bluntly, even coarsely - a repeated study of (the phenomenon that was) Nietzsche rubs off on one; returning to his books again and again over the years, meditating on the details of his relatively short (where sanity is concerned), intensely painful and beautiful life, one cannot but be influenced - 'infected' is perhaps a more honest, if ambiguous, verb - by his intellectual independence, his spiritual sang-froid and his poetic gaiety and melancholy. For Nietzsche was also a great poet, a frequently overlooked fact which has predictably gained him the opprobrium of a veritable host of lesser philosophers who cannot see the advantage poetic expression sometimes holds over reasoned argument unleavened and unilluminated – indeed, unenlivened - by great imagery and lyrical expression.

But a play about Nietzsche? Certainly there are so many ways to go wrong in the endeavour, so many false steps to tread and notes to hit, perhaps prime amongst which must be the inclination clumsily to 'speechify' Nietzsche's thoughts; to insert them in the mouths of various protagonists, erect some vaguely dramatic construction around them and rashly assume the result will cut it as a play.

Fortunately, however, Nietzsche himself comes to the rescue. For his life was not without dramatic incident. Indeed, at several points it was fraught with drama. His father died from a riding accident when Nietzsche was four, the fatherless son then being sent away to undergo many years' rigorous training at the severe but enriching Pforta college.

Later graduating in Philology, he became Basle University's youngest ever professor in that subject, swiftly also becoming (as you do) an intimate of Wagner's inner circle at the same time. When military conflict then threatened to break out between France and Germany, Nietzsche trained as a cavalryman, got invalided out by dint of his own serious riding accident, eventually serving as a medical orderly in the Franco-Prussian war of 1870/1. Thereafter, pensioned off prematurely from his professorship as a result of recurrent illness, Nietzsche travelled in France (somehow avoiding Paris!) and Italy and experienced the travails of intense solitude and, latterly, romantic involvement, falling in love in 1882 with a young woman half his age, the eventually renowned Lou Andreas Salome, with whom he is photographed on the back of this play-script.

Indeed, in the context of the above photo it is perhaps no exaggeration to suggest that one of the unsung traits of Nietzsche's personality is his showmanship. Thankfully there exist several decent photos of Nietzsche at various stages in his life, and in group portraits of him with young friends and acquaintances Nietzsche is frequently the one posed in a more or less contrived Bohemian meditation, manifesting a vaguely 'Young Werther-ish' profile, looking dramatically away from the camera across to some heroic middle-distance as if to say, "I am the one who stands out here; it is I who sense a more profound calling these good fellows do not, cannot hear...'

Then there is the celebrated photograph that, as aforementioned, adorns this cover: say what you will about it, it is clearly not the photograph of a man unused to the spotlight shone by communal good humour. On the contrary, it depicts a man reveling in the theatrical possibilities of social and psycho-sexual absurdity! It is the photograph of a showman – intellectual if not, at times, actual.

If conflict is still the essence of drama (however abstract such discord may occasionally have become in the Modernist canon - one thinks in this context of certain one-man or woman plays, indeed, the whole Beckettian genre in general), then as a playwright I have sought to verbalise Nietzsche's thinking in dialogue only insofar as it directly affects the development of the individuals in the course of the play. In this specific regard, 'show don't tell' has long been paramount amongst Modernist theatrical axioms. Indeed, it is fine as far as it goes - nothing seems more dramatically dated to us now, for example, than a George Bernard Shaw play in which the protagonists exchange long-winded, not to say prolix speeches which seem pompously contrived solely to give vent to the playwright's opinions rather than to reveal the nature and development of the characters themselves. That said, there is a danger in applying our favourite modernist axiom too rigidly. Indeed, we might ask where the great Shakespearian soliloquies would now be had such a 'show, don't tell' principle been unconditionally asserted in his day! The vital point is that certain monologues (or 'soliloquies' or 'speeches' to give them their old-fashioned names) show the evolution of their characters' minds precisely *in the telling*. To this extent, then, the telling *is* the showing.

Lastly, in the process of writing *THHC* I ought to state my constant fear of reducing Nietzsche to the status of a mere foil for yet another predictable romance. Nietzsche was, of course, infinitely more than a mere romantic. That said, his proverbially doomed love for Lou Salome did mark a pivotal point in his artistic, philosophical and spiritual career. Indeed, he was to observe afterwards in a letter 'if I cannot turn even this muck to gold then I am lost...'. To this extent, then, it seemed to me valid to depict Nietzsche as these formidable forces confronted him and impinged both on his common humanity and his uncommon philosophical aspirations. In *THHC*, Nietzsche's obsession with Salome thus becomes the fulcrum upon which he determines the veracity and depth of his own philosophical insights: if they are true and real, then they must prove so at all times, especially, where *THHC* is concerned, under the tumultuous stress of his relationship with Salome. Add to this fact the consideration that it is always fascinating to see how great hearts and minds react under pressure, then you have my motivation for depicting Nietzsche in this way and at this precise time in his life.

Of course, my depiction of Nietzsche is precisely that: a personal one. I think it's probably fair to say that every Nietzsche-lover misconstrues the great man in their own favourite way. This is mine. With a view to creating a dynamic, coherent plot for the play I have, for example, indulged in certain chronological eccentricities and historical distortions. Nietzsche's aristocratic, young disciple Heinrich Von Holstein never actually met Lou Salome, whose lover he is in the drama; additionally, it was Paul Rée who ultimately ran off with her. However, I trust that in riding rough-shod over certain (minor) facts in my attempt to bring Nietzsche's personality to life, the play ultimately arrives at a much greater poetic verisimilitude.

Here, it must be added that in the space of a play one can only hope to cover a small proportion of the major philosophical issues Nietzsche raises. Instead, then, of any foredoomed, compendious ambition, I have instinctively opted for an impressionistic characterization of Nietzsche that seeks to portray his mind in the act of conceiving and discussing a few of the subjects which (I consider) constitute his main areas of intellectual and spiritual concern. In the crime of confidence I have committed in daring to re-create his character in this way, I have been aided and abetted to a large extent by having visited at least some of the emotional staging posts the great thinker stopped at on his philosophical pilgrimage. Blessed and cursed with the poet's sensibility, with all its incumbent yearnings, its exhilarating moments of vision and painful periods of blindness, I have experienced what it is like to leave one's own country to live abroad (in my case in Italy), and to endure the predictable but still nonetheless overpoweringly strange solitude and loneliness of the émigré.

In such a context, to say goodbye to one's old self is to greet one's new self. I mark the beginning of my own evolution as a man on the day - and moment - I turned and looked at Dover's White Cliffs receding in the distance as the channel ferry drew me towards my first long stay in Italy way back in the summer of 1984. That personal pilgrimage would not have been possible without the love and companionship of Joanna Jones (as she then was, before the later bout of insanity under whose influence she was to consent to become my wife). Such, indeed, is the power and purpose of spiritual friendship: its participants cooperate in sun and rain over the years to raise the architecture of each other's aspirations, confronting problems as they arise, from the minutest details to the large logistical problems; from the hopeful drawing board to the happy grand design, so to speak. To Joanna, then, this play is dedicated with delight and gratitude.

Acknowledgements

To Jo, again, further, more precise gratitude is due. Firstly, as an editor she flourishes a scalpel with brilliant, unflappable, surgical accuracy; no less importantly in this case, as a director her insight has proved priceless. On first reading any new work she is quiet, studious and thoughtful; on a second, more expressively ruminative; on a third, thrillingly articulate, as she brings into play a whole host of dramatic ideas with which to realise the implicit dynamic of scenes and improve the flow of dialogue. No playwright could enjoy more creative counsel!

To Jack Murphy, for sharpening my wits about the deeper philosophical implications of Darwinism, for his general criticism and for his brilliant design of THHC's book cover, I offer my delighted thanks!

To Marcus Fellowes, the same is due. For his invaluable energy in pursuit of editorial and IT competence and for his companionship over cappuccinos in fair and foul weather, I am indeed indebted! For his unswerving proof-reading perfectionism, I also offer sincerest posthumous gratitude to my friend Dominic Adams, tragically taken from us since the first edition of this play was published. I'm sure we'll meet again, Dom.

To Hell in a Handcart

*"To those human beings who are of any concern to me
I wish suffering, desolation, sickness, ill-treatment, indignities - I wish
that they should not remain unfamiliar with profound self-contempt, the
torture of self-mistrust, the wretchedness of the vanquished: I have no
pity for them, because I wish them the only thing that can prove today
whether one is worth anything or not - that one endures."*

(F. Nietzsche - The Will to Power, p. 481)

Cast

Friedrich Nietzsche – philosopher, late 30s.

Paul Rée – Nietzsche's friend, also a philosopher, mid 30s.

Lou Andreas Salome – poetess, aged 20.

Heinrich Von Holstein – poet, mid-20s, her lover.

Elisabeth Nietzsche – Nietzsche's sister, mid 30s.

A studio photographer (can be doubled by actor playing Rée)

Production notes.

The play takes place over two acts, shifting scene from Genoa in the first to Sils Maria in the Swiss Alps in the second. Staging should be simple with minimum clutter. Lighting design is key in recreating the contrast of moods between the Mediterranean and the Alpine.

Note re: music.

Throughout the play, soft Chopin piano music of varying moods (not his more melodramatic pieces) link the scenes

Act 1. Sc. 1

*Genoa. Nietzsche's study. Night. Nietzsche stands at his window
gazing at an, as yet distant, electric storm. Lightning flickers without
thunder. Suddenly we see Nietzsche wince and clutch his head in
some pain. Momentarily rocked off balance, he holds onto the table.
Slowly righting himself, he goes to his desk where he composes
himself. As the lightning continues to flicker, Nietzsche begins to
write in silence. In voice-over he narrates the following:*

NIETZ: I write by lightning – only as many words as I can see to
write… only, that is, as long as the lightning lasts: my beautiful,
inverted lightning, my jagged black ink upon a white sheet of sky.
Forgive my aristocratic immodesty, which, I know, is not to the taste of
the age; but one should never write under any provocation but that of
inspiration. What other power could light up our night-sky, our dark
interior landscape? And then not without a certain suicidal danger; since
the poet must stand in the open to attract the lightning, which blasts him
just as destructively as any solitary tree in the landscape. Be warned,
then, fellow storm-hunters: the pen is a perilous lightning conductor: he
who holds it stands to be turned to ashes….

More lightning. Nietzsche rises from seat, gazes from window. Fade.

1.2

*Nietzsche's room. Next morning. Sunlight pierces three-quarters
drawn curtains. A Chopin nocturne dies away. The room's one
apparent extravagance is its piano, otherwise it is simply furnished
with a desk, a chaise, a chair, a loaded bookshelf on which glasses
and a water jug rest. One wall has a sequence of tatty lists pinned to it,
several of which have dropped to litter the floor. Nietzsche sits at the
piano as his sister, Elizabeth, tidies up. He plays slow, simple chords.*

ELIZ: You play so beautifully, Fritz; what is that tune? *(he stops)*

NIETZ: You mean, what *was* that tune?

He rises, goes to his desk, picks up a book.

ELIZ: Why are you in such a bad mood?

NIETZ: I'm not in a bad mood – at least I *wasn't*.

ELIZ: You are! I'm only here for a week: you might at least be civil. *(Beat)* Actually, I can't think why you moved here. Yes, I know it's cheaper, but Nice is so much fresher... cleaner. I suppose I'm biased: I love French style, it seems to run through the whole of their society: even the poodles walk with their noses in the air. It's shocking really, the difference between the two countries. All this unification nonsense, Italy's falling down in my opinion: buildings peeling, roads pot-holed; and the smell! Everything's decaying...

NIETZ: I like decay! - and to hell with unification, the whole of Europe is falling apart: Italians are just more honest about it.

ELIZ: Well I can do without that kind of honesty. In fact if that's honesty, give me a bit of artful French deception. *(Beat)* You ought to know there are unpleasant rumours going around, Friedrich *(beat)* among the guests at the hotel.

NIETZ: Really. And who are that venerable sect of dodderers and whores getting their false teeth into?

ELIZ: You.

NIETZ: Me? They must be bored.

ELIZ: Well, I care even if you don't! You're my brother and I can't just stand by and listen to it.

NIETZ: Then leave the room.

ELIZ: Be serious, Friedrich! It's your reputation we're talking about!

NIETZ: You mean I have one?

ELIZ: You won't have if you carry on working with that Jew.

NIETZ: *(wearily)* Please don't call him that.

ELIZ: Well he is, isn't he?

NIETZ: He's Jewish, yes.

ELIZ: Then he's a Jew.

NIETZ: Yes, but not in the way you mean.

ELIZ: Your association with him ruins your prospects.

NIETZ: I don't *have* any prospects; I don't *want* any prospects. I'm quite happy with my life as it is – unlike some people.

ELIZ: - And as for introducing you to that girl: you'd be mad to form any kind of association with her, Friedrich; scandal follows her wherever she goes.

NIETZ: What, like one of those ridiculous French poodles you're so fond of! Look, Elizabeth, if you wouldn't mind; I really should write. I'll call you a cab.

ELIZ: Don't bother.

She picks up her cape and is about to flounce out, then turns.

Friedrich, I only want what's best for you. I'm here to help!

NIETZ: I don't need any help.

ELIZ: No, well remind me of that when it comes to your manuscripts. Last time I seem to remember you pleading for my help deciphering your damned writing. *(Beat)* Fritz, don't be angry with me.

NIETZ: I'm not angry with you: I just wish to do some work.

ELIZ: Promise me you'll get some rest at some stage.

NIETZ: Yes, yes, I'll rest.

ELIZ: You won't. You never do: you work too hard and then your eyesight gets worse, and that makes the headaches come back. You know what the doctor said.

NIETZ: Doctors! Last one you brought looked like a murderer - *was* a murderer! If I'd carried on with that poison he recommended... I can look after myself.

ELIZ: Then promise me you will. I mean it: you're the only 'genius' brother I've got. – Well...?

NIETZ: I promise.

ELIZ: Good. Then I'll see you tomorrow. *(Calls out as she leaves)* Good luck with your work! *(Exit)*

NIETZ: *(to himself)* I don't need luck, my dear sister... *(rises)* I just need you... to go away – preferably to another country.

He goes to the curtains, opens them a bit wider to ensure that she's gone, then returns and sits at the piano. He plays a chord or two, only to be interrupted by urgent knocking on the door. Enter Nietzsche's friend Rée, taking off his jacket and serving himself a glass of water.

REE: Was that your sister I just saw? - Gave me the blackest look!

NIETZ: She doesn't like Jews.

REE: Nor do I, and I *am* one! Ghastly race; but then aren't they all? Humankind en masse: not a pretty sight! Your sister and I should have a talk: sounds like we've got a lot in common.

NIETZ: She thinks you should be deported.

REE: Where to? America? Egypt! Now I *do* want to see the pyramids before I die. No, hold on: they don't like Jews there either - and it's too hot. Mind you, no hotter than it is here: unbearable out there today.

Rée pours another glass of water, Nietzsche pours a glass for himself. Rée paces about.

NIETZ: The heat is setting in: I shan't stay here much longer. I meant to leave a week ago. Sit down for god's sake, you're making me nervous.

REE: I can't. I'm far too excited.

Rée goes to the window.

Can't we open these curtains?

NIETZ: I'd rather you didn't - my eyes aren't good today: a bit later when the sun's moved round.

REE: Of course, I'm sorry.

NIETZ: No, no: it's me who should apologise: forcing my visitors to live in the dark like bats!

REE: Yes, it is a bit of a cave in here – but a philosopher's cave! Good old Plato: where would we be without him?

NIETZ: Yet, where are we *with* the old Greek fraud, eh?

REE: Ha, where indeed?

NIETZ: Stupefied by two and half thousand years of charming nonsense, that's where: life is vicious and transient therefore we must escape into a world of heavenly forms. Why? Personally, I don't see the need!

Rée takes off his jacket and unbuttons his shirt.

REE: Absolutely! What's wrong with things being vicious and meaningless?

NIETZ: I didn't say 'meaningless! My point, Rée, as you well know, is that what you see in life has an ironic habit of turning out to be precisely what you get; the question is why *do* you see what you see? Plato was a barren fantasist. Dionysus is the perfect counterweight: I'm currently working his chaos ---

REE: Fritz, Fritz, I've only just finished breakfast, it's far too early for dialectic!

NIETZ: What time is it?

REE: Ten thirty – ish.

NIETZ: - Ish?

REE: All right: ten thirty three...

NIETZ: Then the sun will be off the front of the building in about... seventeen minutes. - Yes, I know it's obsessive... only reason I took this dismal apartment: cypresses block out the light before nine and then good old Helios's chariot disappears round the Eastern corner just before 11.

REE: - Ish...

NIETZ: Ish... *(The men embrace)* – It's good to see you Paul.

REE: You too my dear, dear friend. *(Rée goes to sit down but then changes his mind.)*

It's no good, Fritz, I can't contain myself: we're on the verge of something wonderful – I feel it!

NIETZ: And feelings never lie.

REE: Ah mock all you want, but you wait til you meet her: she's perfect.

NIETZ: Sounds ominous.

REE: Heinrich is bringing her: *without* that ridiculous Bavarian chaperone, if they can give her the slip.

NIETZ: Heinrich?

REE: Yes, turns out they already know each other - met last year in St Petersburg; of course, he's completely smitten with her. He didn't mention it before because you didn't know her then. - You don't know her *now*; oh but Fritz you're about to! Then you'll see what we're all going on about. You've got a major surprise in store. She'll change all your ideas.

NIETZ: I doubt it.

REE: About women, I mean.

NIETZ: As I say: I doubt it.

REE: Well, you know what they say: doubt is the father of revelation!

NIETZ: *Do* they say that?

REE: No, I just made it up, but it's true. Oh I know you're sceptical, but this can work! Why should it not? People of like minds working together, living together… we could buy a cat!

NIETZ: What's a cat got to do with anything?

REE: Animals exert a benign influence, Friedrich, especially on philosophers. Cats are very calming.

NIETZ: What if I don't want to be calm!

REE: Then we'll buy a Spaniel! You could tire it out on those ridiculously long walks you do! Look, stop being so contrary, anyone'd think you didn't want this to work. *(Beat)* But listen to me: I'm being completely insensitive: I haven't even asked you about your health, your infernal migraine: how have you been? Actually, that's another thing that'll be cured by the right kind of company: I'm convinced those migraines are the result of too much solitude. Yes, I know solitude is vital, but not uninterrupted: man isn't meant to be alone: we are social animals.

NIETZ: Then why do we drive each other mad within half an hour of being with each other? Present company excepted of course. No, I'm afraid solitude is here to stay: but on what terms, that's the question: as

(Nietzsche cont.)

an occasional welcome guest, or a poisonous presence we can't get rid of.

REE: Fritz ---

NIETZ: Of course, one's own mood predetermines everything. Take this morning; I mean before my sister came, obviously: I felt perfectly happy just sitting writing; I didn't even feel alone: the spirit of my work accompanied me: like one of those daemons Socrates rambles on about! But the moment I put down the pen I become another person altogether. I fidget, I look around for something to do: everything feels oppressive. I feel utterly hemmed in by the things in the room, by life itself. I can't wait to get out into the street, just to see another human being. Pathetic, isn't it? A man who can't bear his own company!

REE: My dear Friedrich, I couldn't agree less! Look, it's not natural to live in isolation: we both know that. We've been talking for months about a community, well now we can have – *shall* have a community.

NIETZ: Four is not a community.

REE: It's a start. Anyway, it's five, with your sister.

NIETZ: No! I've told you: I cannot live with my sister: she can visit, but that's it.

REE: All right, all right. Four then. Anyway, we don't need your sister. Listen, Friedrich, this young woman - I don't say this lightly, but she's the answer to our prayers.

NIETZ: Poor girl.

REE: Yes, she's young, but wise beyond her years. And wildly independent. If I hadn't heard it with my own ears I wouldn't't've believed it. 'I've been reading a revolutionary book by Nietzsche', she said - stopped me in my tracks. - Stopped her in hers when I told her I knew you! As much as I could do to prevent her coming over immediately. She's impulsive to the point of recklessness.

NIETZ: Recklessness is good: I like reckless.

REE: But sensitive too. She's a vegetarian – now, don't take that the wrong way! The cast of her mind is almost entirely in sympathy with our way of thinking.

NIETZ: Almost?

REE: Well she has some interesting ideas about equality, but we'll knock those out of her: she's dangerously logical for a woman, I promise you!

NIETZ: Reckless, sensitive *and* logical: I like her more with every passing paradox.

REE: But above all, poetic!

NIETZ: You had to ruin it, didn't you. Anything but 'poetic!' Just a pretty word for being confused about everything.

REE: *You* write poetically.

NIETZ: Only when I've got a headache – which is far too often, I concede. Actually, I love poetry: It's just poets I can't stand.

REE: Well you'll love this one – and she'll love you. I tell you she's the most exquisite young woman, Friedrich! Actually, the word 'woman' doesn't really do her justice: she's more of a…spirit; like an angel: androgynous! Come to think of it, she does have something quite masculine as well as feminine about her.

NIETZ: And which side are you in love with, Rée ?

REE: Both, of course! And you will be too!

NIETZ: *(wearily)* Yes, well, you've given the poor girl such a write-up she can't fail to disappoint. Perhaps we'd better just get this meeting over and done with.

REE: We will: she'll be here in twenty minutes.

NIETZ What? You said after lunch!

REE: That was before I met her this morning: she can't make this afternoon.

NIETZ: Well, I can't possibly see her this morning! I don't see people in the morning – you know that!

REE: You're seeing me.

NIETZ: That's because you barged in here unannounced.

REE: I know, I know: I didn't have time to warn you. Anyway, what's wrong with a little surprise? You shouldn't let your time be so damned structured. You know what's missing from your life? The spirit of devilry! Stop trying to control everything! Look at all these lists! *(Goes up to the wall of lists)* Lists of books to read; composers, concertos to listen to; lists of ideas! Shopping lists! Look at this one! *(starts to read)*

NIETZ: My dear Rée ---

REE: 'Five thirty a.m: get up, circumambulate garden.' – Who in their right mind goes 'circumambulating' at 5.30?

NIETZ: I'm *not* in my right mind - thank god. Give that to me!

REE: 'Six a.m: light breakfast of nuts and milk.' – Nuts and milk? What are you: a goblin, a savage foraging for food in the forest?

NIETZ: Philosophically speaking - yes.

REE: 'Seven o'clock: light reading' – Light reading? You don't *read* any light books!

NIETZ: I don't know: some of yours are pretty flimsy.

REE: *(sarcastic)* Ha ha.. – 'eight o'clock: swim followed by 20 minute rest on rocks... - eat at Jacques' in Cap Ferat!' Cap Ferat? That's 100 miles away, what do you do, catch a dolphin?

NIETZ: That's a French list: I keep the ones that work.

REE: What do you mean 'work'?

NIETZ: The ones that seem to help me.

REE: Help you what?

NIETZ: Organise myself! I don't know... unburden my mind. Lists help me regulate my energies - you wouldn't understand. Anyway, I don't keep to them. I break them when I want to. I'm not tyrannised by them, as you insist on believing.

REE: You *are*.

NIETZ: *(pantomime)* Oh no I'm not.

REE: Then tear them up.

NIETZ: Don't be absurd.

REE: Go on. I'll do it for you.

NIETZ: Take your hands off them!

REE: I'm tearing them.

NIETZ: I said leave them alone.

REE: Here goes the first one...

NIETZ: For god's sake! *(He snatches them angrily from Rée and throws them in the bin himself)*.

REE: There. That wasn't so hard, was it?

NIETZ: Are you specifically trying to be infantile today? Because I confess you're succeeding magnificently.

REE: What if I am: it's the effect Signorina Salome has on me – on every man.

NIETZ: Then may I suggest she's not quite the good influence you propose.

REE: *(beat)* She's very pretty.

NIETZ: I'm not interested in her looks.

REE: Of course you are: all men are interested in a woman's looks.

NIETZ: I'm not all men.

REE: Well Signorina Salome's not all women either: that's why you'll get on famously. I tell you it'll be love at first sight.

NIETZ: Oh for god's sake! No it won't, Rée, love may be blind but *I* am not, I assure you.

REE: Yes you *are*... - Well you are without those goldfish bowls you call glasses.

NIETZ: I can see clearly enough to recognise a fool when I see one: when you say love, what you mean is obsession.

REE: Ten minutes. *(Nietzsche looks questioningly)* She'll be here in ten minutes. And then you'll be obsessed too.

Nietzsche sits down, takes up a book, reads for a second or two then casts it aside and rises irritably.

NIETZ: Look this is all quite ridiculous. I can't possibly entertain a young lady like this!

REE: Like what?

NIETZ: With you sitting here – like some damned procurer.

REE: I beg your pardon.

NIETZ: She must think I'm some sort of impotent old degenerate who can't arrange his own meetings with women.

REE: She thinks nothing of the sort: for god's sake calm down. *(Beat)* If anything's procured Miss Salome's interest in you, it's your books.

NIETZ: What does she say about them? No, don't tell me: I'm not interested. *(Beat)* Did she like Daybreak? No, what does she say about The Wanderer: I signed that book in blood; if she likes that we'll get on.

REE: She loved it.

NIETZ: Did she? What did she love about it?

REE: Everything.

NIETZ: What specifically?

REE: The style: she mentioned your prose style specifically!

NIETZ: Prose style!? Yes, s'pose it cuts a dash. Why not? Style is truth making an entrance: the 'bella figura' of the new, – what else did she like?

REE: Fritz, your rod is showing.

NIETZ: What?

REE: You're fishing for compliments in the most obvious way.

NIETZ: Am I?

REE: She said she'd never read anything so intellectually independent in her life.

NIETZ: Hardly surprising, she's only twenty-one.

REE: And yet she's read your books already.

NIETZ: True; the girl must have spirit.

REE: In abundance, I assure you.

NIETZ: Still, I can't meet her – not this morning, not like this.

REE: Then you'll never meet her.

NIETZ: Why not?

REE: Because her mother is taking her back to Paris tomorrow, and from there back to Moscow a week later. Fritz, meetings like this are once in a lifetime; she's only in Genoa for a week, and she's desperate to meet you. Look, when she comes I'm going to leave you two together --- no, hear me out! It's vital you have time to meet each other first as individuals - no-one else around; not me, not Von Holstein.

Sound of door-bell.

There she is! – I'll go and get her.

Exit Rée. Nietzsche goes to the mirror, straightens his moustache, hair, glasses, etc. Goes to sit, posed in relaxed position, in chair; hears the approach of voices off-stage, suddenly rises and stands, again posed, in relaxed fashion by the window, holding an open book. Then just as Rée, Heinrich and Lou Salome enter he hurls the book onto the sofa. She smiles as it sails past her.

REE: Fritz, allow me to introduce fräulein Lou Andreas Salome; - fräulein Salome, Herr Friedrich Nietzsche.

Nietzsche bows and kisses her hand.

NIETZ: Gnädiges fräulein, I have waited a long time for this pleasure – perhaps a whole lifetime.

LOU: That long! Then how can I fail to disappoint you, Herr Nietzsche!

Nietzsche and Rée exchange an ironic glance as Lou extends a hand which Nietzsche kisses gracefully.

NIETZ: Your presence alone is sufficient to allay any disillusionment.

Slightly embarrassing pause. She recovers her poise and looks round the room.

HEIN: We had a hell of a job getting here, I don't mind telling you: a horse collapsed in the promenade.

REE: Poor old thing, flogged to death by its damnable driver, no doubt: I saw some appalling treatment yesterday...

HEIN: Whole street was blocked! Queue right back to the Porta Alpina.

LOU: *(softly but distinctly)* It wasn't dead.

HEIN: Italians shouting and cursing each other, trying to pull the poor beast out of the way so the trams could get through. And then Lou got out and started cursing them too.

LOU: It wasn't dead! I just wanted to... comfort it in its last moments.

HEIN: She made those Italians back off, I can tell you. Swore at them like a fishwife! I blush to recall it.

REE: I can't believe that.

HEIN: In Italian too!

LOU: *(distractedly)* And German. – The Latins are not good with animals...

NIETZ: No, indeed... but then we North Europeans are not good with people...

LOU: At least we don't flog them to death.

NIETZ: Not in public, perhaps: we have factories to disguise our systems of slavery. Tell me, fräulein: did the horse die peacefully, as you wished?

LOU: I don't know. It didn't close its eyes – when it died...

HEIN: She just kept stroking the poor creature's neck: Italians shouting, jostling each other, and right there in the middle of it: Lou and the poor creature: quite an image, I can tell you.

LOU: Then they came and dragged it off - like a piece of meat.

HEIN: That's all animals are to Italians: meat.

REE: To be served up on the dishes of filthy tratorrie the same evening no doubt!

HEIN: Disgusting the way they eat horsemeat!

LOU: I don't eat any meat

NIETZ: Why not?

LOU: Because it smells of death.

NIETZ: *(beat)* What's wrong with death..?

Faint embarrassment, which Lou punctures.

LOU: This is a beautiful room. I love these Genoese proportions: the ceilings are high, but not too high.

NIETZ: I hate tall ceilings: they make me feel ---

LOU: Suffocated by too much space.

NIETZ: Exactly! I must have a room that nourishes a sense of human proportion – Vitruvian man and all that! Anything too big, I feel vulnerable, I can't protect my thoughts from distraction.

LOU: And yet you love the mountains…

NIETZ: Ah, yes, well…

LOU: I mean your books are full of references to them, to the perspectives they confer: no doubt it's difficult *not* to condemn mankind when one looks down on him from a height of ten thousand feet.

NIETZ: *(somewhat taken aback)* Indeed.

Lou starts to take off her long summer lace coat.

REE: I'm so sorry, you must be sweltering - let me take…

She has already left it on his outstretched arm.

LOU: And yet in all your books, well, those I've read, there seems to be, correct me if I'm wrong, a sense that you also fear the mountains...

NIETZ: Yes, indeed, depends on my appetite for solitude – and my mood - but then what doesn't? Ambivalence is the key in which the music of human nature is set, is it not, fräulein? Well, my nature at any rate: I never feel one thing, but another part of me can put a case for the other side.

REE: Fritz could argue with his own shadow, Lou, I assure you!

NIETZ: And frequently do! The dialogue never ceases to fascinate.

LOU: Well, may I say it is my respectful wish to sit in on your conversations and take a few notes.

NIETZ: No, no, interrupt as often as you like! I've been talking to myself for far too long! God knows, I'm the only one who'll listen!

They all smile ruefully. Lou goes to the window and starts to open the curtains. Nietzsche turns away.

LOU: It's so dark in here: do you mind?

REE: *(anxiously)* I think you'll find they let in too much light!

LOU: No, the sun went round the side of the building as I came in. I always notice that sort of thing, I'm a sun-worshipper, I'm afraid. - Look: see? Quite disappeared.

Sure enough, the opened curtains admit only a gentle light. Nietzsche relaxes.

For you, it's space, Herr Nietzsche; for me, it's sunlight. I know it's neurotic but I can't stand wasting a second of sunny weather.

REE: It's not neurotic: it's the sign of a healthy disposition seeking the light ---

NIETZ: - And avoiding its own shadow, perhaps.... *(He is clearly enrapt by her)*

REE: Well, look, we've one or two things to do, as I said.

HEIN: Have we?

REE: Yes! So you won't mind if we leave you two to get better acquainted. – A word of warning: Fritz is conducting a one-man war on Plato. Do yourself a favour: don't get caught in the crossfire.

LOU: I'll keep my head down.

REE: Then we'll see you both later.

HEIN: But ---

REE: But, nothing, Heinrich, I need your advice...

The two men exit with Rée chivvying Heinrich out.

LOU: Poor Rée, he's so desperate for us to get on.

NIETZ: He needn't have worried. Really, Miss Salome ---

LOU: 'Lou'...

NIETZ: Yes... - Forgive my forwardness but it's such a pleasure to meet someone with whom one feels such an immediate sympathy.... I hope you don't mind me saying this, but absurd as it sounds, somehow I feel we've known each other for a long time.

LOU: Perhaps we have. In another life.

NIETZ: I feel sure of it. Don't the Hindus and Buddhists believe in reincarnation!

LOU: And Plato too.

NIETZ: Yes, even that old fraud couldn't deny the idea has a certain poetry.

LOU: Much as he tried to boil everything down to reason.

NIETZ: And what sort of mind would want to do that – even if it *could* be done, which it can't!

LOU: And even if it were true – which it isn't!

NIETZ: Hear, hear! To hell with Plato!

They laugh modestly as the 'ice is broken,' etc.

LOU: So Rée is serious, then: you *are* waging war on Plato?

NIETZ: Not this morning. This afternoon I might take a pot-shot at the old shyster; god knows, he's a difficult man to kill, philosophically-speaking: every time you think you've got him, up he pops again! Can't keep a good corpse down!

LOU: Even one that's been dead for two thousand years.

NIETZ: Especially those! Being dead's so charismatic! Look at us, still discussing Plato and his ridiculous forms two and a half thousand years after the old fantasist croaked. I ask you, what do they even mean, what *could* they mean? How could the 'form of the good' exist apart from the reality of goodness, of a so-called 'good' act? There, you see: you've got me going. Ah Miss Salome, there's so much to talk about!

LOU: And yet Rée tells me you're heading North.

NIETZ: Yes *(beat)* in more ways than one.... If I could stay I would: I belong here: the moment I set foot on southern soil something in me wakes. The Latin certainty of a flawless summer's day: time flows more easily. One doesn't grab at life so nervously. The sun pours out endless amounts of gold: one can waste it and still feel rich. And it's a physical thing: I feel the light replenish me: I arrive empty-hearted from the North - a couple of days later the glass is full again.

LOU: Then why leave just as summer's beginning?

NIETZ: I don't want to: I have to. *(Beat)* I have a theory – I know it sounds stupid: it's to do with barometric pressure. Over the past few years my calculations reveal, in relation to the local geography, I mean - the pressure outside equates to…exerts an equivalent pressure in ---

LOU: The heat gives you headaches…

NIETZ: Yes, yes… *(slightly embarrassed silence)* Anyway, summer's well and truly here: to the mountains I must go: not that they're without their own challenge, as you suggested. Mountains are extremely unforgiving.

LOU: Of what?

NIETZ: *(beat)* Any false motive for solitude…. I find I must gather myself together every year to face them again. In fact, every time I leave I go through this pathetic period of regret; I start feeling ridiculously well-disposed to everyone.

LOU: Everyone?

NIETZ: It's true: fruit-sellers in the street, tramps, aristocrats in carriages: they all suddenly take on a rosy hue just as I'm about to leave. It's a sure sign it's time to go. I get impossibly sentimental about the human race.

LOU: Even women?

NIETZ: Especially women.

LOU: And Rée said you were a misogynist…

NIETZ: Not true: I detest men and women equally. Usually! - Actually I don't. It may come as a surprise to you Fräulein ---

LOU: Lou.

NIETZ: Lou – that actually I love my fellow man – and woman. In fact, it's because I love them that I detest what they they've allowed themselves to become.

LOU: Which is?

NIETZ: Average. *(Beat)* Politely, poisonously average. Democracy, what is it but government by a majority of fools over a minority of fools! We wanted it, well now we've got it - *(acknowledging her protest)* – half the human race excepted. But women'll find out soon enough: democracy's a sickness not a cure. It propagates mediocrity: newspapers reek of the contagion – all of us drowning in the shit of petty opinions. Spewing them out like sewage into a great stinking sea – forgive my vehemence, but it's no wonder we make ourselves sick. We need a good war to purge us.

LOU: Of what?

NIETZ: Our triviality - all that bourgeois morality. The terror of giving offence! The outrage! - Tonic water for invalids. Morally speaking, people get the diseases they deserve.

LOU: And the gods?

Nietzsche is momentarily disarmed by her sudden change of conversational direction.

NIETZ: Yes, them too.

LOU: Which is why your philosophy cures us of religion.

NIETZ: You flatter me. Religion can't be cured, it's in our blood – like malaria.

LOU: And yet they say you killed god.

NIETZ: Don't blame me! God died of his own absurdity decades ago; my books merely record the time and place of death.

LOU: Like a coroner.

NIETZ: Ha! a coroner of dead ideas… I'll settle for that. Tell me: do *you* go to church?

LOU: No, not since I was seven.

NIETZ: There you are: God is dead for you. But I'll bet he still lingers on, like an ogre in your conscience!

LOU: I confess I do cross myself when I enter a cathedral.

NIETZ: Exactly! That's just it: we have to grow up, find new ideals!

LOU: Maybe some of us possess a less naive conception of god.

NIETZ: Then share it! Because we're going to need it, I assure you. Literary irony apart, God's death is the most terrible thing that's ever happened to us. The death of the sacred! We need something to adore, Miss Salome; something we can't find in each other! Some love of something beautiful, terrifying, something that... purifies us... - or there'll be the devil to pay, I can assure you. Killing your gods is not a good thing to do – unless you've got something better to replace them with... Ah it's impossible to talk about these things without sounding like a zealot oneself!

LOU: Sound perfectly reasonable to me!

NIETZ: *(Warms to his theme again)* All I mean is that life without a higher meaning is vile - a mere marketplace for buying and selling.

LOU: Run by a nation of shopkeepers!

NIETZ: Yes! Viva Napoleon! Whatever the English may think, the soul is more than a salesman.

LOU: So what *is* the sacred?

NIETZ: Ah there you have it: forget 'to be or not to be' Miss Salome: *that's* the question for *our* age! You might help me find an answer... – were you to come and join us, that is... *(beat)* Rée, Von Holstein and me, I mean – not that we'd all be living in each other's pockets. The idea is to give each other time and space, not just to write, but to live these questions! To guard each other's solitude.

LOU: You use that word a lot.

NIETZ: Yes, forgive me: I'm becoming old-fashioned, which is unforgivable in an age of fashion. Ideas must have novelty, style. Sadly, there's nothing less fashionable than solitude. Solitude is the opposite of everything cheap. Actually, it's the opposite of everything - except perhaps death…

LOU: Then it's also the opposite of life.

NIETZ: And yet everything worthwhile comes from it: poetry, painting, music – even philosophy, god help us!

LOU: Love? Does that come from solitude?

NIETZ: A purer form of it. One not coarsened by desire.

LOU: Coarsened?

NIETZ: Well, of course, we're propagated by desire… *(She laughs)* why are you laughing?

LOU: The word 'propagate' in connection with love!

NIETZ: I didn't say 'love'…

LOU: I did. Desire is part of love.

NIETZ: Yes, well - If I confuse philosophy with love it's because you make me… *(Breaks off)* - weren't we talking about solitude?

LOU: We moved on to love.

NIETZ: Did we. Well anyway, when we say 'solitude' what we really mean is a quality of silence that one can experience anywhere; however many people are around… *(Beat)* You know what I'm talking about. You know what solitude is: I can see it in your eyes.

LOU: *What* can you see?

NIETZ: The necessary poison of self-doubt.

LOU: Necessary?

NIETZ: One drinks it in solitude – like a truth serum; without it no real questions are asked – not that the answers are always pleasant.... *(Beat)* Dark times are coming, Miss Salome. Things are breaking up. We call the dissolution progress because it flatters us to do so. But we're part of the decline. We *are* the decline. *(Beat)* Of course, there's nothing we can do to stop it! I wouldn't want to stop it. The forces ranged against us are all necessary: like Greek furies, they're here to take revenge. *(Abruptly, Nietzsche lightens up)* And talking of furies, Rée tells me you are a great champion of your gender; equality and all that.

LOU: Why not? Why should you impose your will on me? Why would you *need* to? Unless you felt threatened, of course.

NIETZ: What man *doesn't* feel threatened by a powerful woman?

LOU: Actually, I don't rate equality as a concept. I don't identify myself wholly with my sex – either sex. *(Beat)* I want to be myself. Whatever that means. *(Beat)* That's where you come in, Herr Nietzsche.

NIETZ: Me? What can I do?

LOU: Show me the way. You're a guide, are you not?

NIETZ: I have enough trouble making my own way in life, and not just metaphorically, I assure you; blind as I am without these damn things. Excuse me...

He takes off his glasses to wipe them.

LOU: How much can you see without them? That is, if you don't mind me asking such a personal question.

NIETZ: No, no; ask me anything you like, the more personal the better! *(He gazes at her)* I can see you are an attractive young woman, but just how young and how attractive I couldn't say – without my glasses.

LOU: Then you had better continue to look at me *without* your glasses.

NIETZ: Too late: I already know the truth.

LOU: Which is?

NIETZ: That you are attractive enough to make a nuisance of yourself.

 LOU: Is that how you see attraction between the sexes?

NIETZ: Insofar as it leads to collisions, yes.

LOU: Collisions can be avoided.

NIETZ: By what?

LOU: Mediation... by the spirit of love.

NIETZ: That word again! If I knew what you meant by it I might argue with you about it. But then I'm just a crusty old philosopher, I wouldn't know what love was if I saw it.

LOU: You don't *see* love, you *feel* it.

NIETZ: Touché! I submit to love's deft rapier.

LOU: Then put down the shield of your solitude – just for a moment.

NIETZ: A pleasure; never has anything weighed so heavy with me. I've lost my sense of balance, you see. Maybe that's something *you* can teach *me*: the moment solitude tips into loneliness: I'd be most grateful. *(Beat)* May I confess one thing to you Lou? – What you said earlier about solitude: I have a great fear that all my work, the whole of my philosophy can be reduced to that one damned word. Why should anything so necessary be so painful? We're born alone, we die alone; why is it so terrifying to *live* alone? *(Beat)*

LOU: You said you knew the answer....

NIETZ: *(deadpan)* We don't exist *(beat)* without each other. I said solitude is a truth serum – it's more like hemlock. Too much solitude is a slow death: you lose your identity; nothing confirms who you are: you might as well die - you *do* die. Yes nature is beautiful, but after a while it gives nothing back; a mountains has no emotions, no feeling for you... and the soul needs food just as much as the body.... Not that cities are any better: there's no cruelty like the noise of crowds. If every man and woman shunned you in the street, how long do you think you'd last before you went mad? An hour? A day? Two days? You'd beg for mercy. *(Beat)* Foreign cities are poems of oblivion: in Rome I spoke to no-one for weeks. Not one real conversation... some days a smile from a beggar, a prostitute, a doorman was the only thing that kept me sane. Loneliness erases you: all you see is your shadow in shop windows. *(Beat)* What do you see when you look in the mirror Lou?

LOU: Me? - I see a young woman searching for someone, something.

NIETZ: And I recognise her! We're mirrors! Desires, fears reflected in each other's faces – like credentials we accept or reject. Miss Lou Andreas Salome, poetess! mystic! Professor Nietzsche, doctor of philology! Philosopher! Really? Only if you believe me. To maintain faith in oneself when no-one else does: the most difficult thing in the world... *(beat)* I write to communicate because if I *don't*, I fear my face might disappear in the mirror... *(beat)* Yes, of course, we must learn to live alone - but only with each other's help.... That's what friendship is: not a substitute for solitude: - a place to *practise* it! An arena! Everything is a preparation for solitude.

LOU: Even Love?

NIETZ: Especially love! Have you seen that Greek painting 'The divers Tomb'? It's in Paestum! I'll take you there. Promise me you won't go with anyone but me!

LOU: Promise ---

NIETZ: He's in mid-air – the diver! *That's* how to die! Diving into solitude. Sun above! Sea below! But the platform from which he dives: that stillness, confidence: that comes, it *must* come from the confidence of love; friendship that fortifies us... however terrifying the silence gets.

LOU: Because the same silence that threatens to destroy you also transforms you...

NIETZ: *(Stopped in his tracks)* Yes...

Silence. She takes his hand. They do not speak as Nietzsche takes his hand gently away and goes to the window.

NIETZ: I'm going to Sils Maria, but that needn't stop us being together! All of us, I mean. There are plenty of houses available! Rée knows it well: he visits me there, Heinrich too.

LOU: Then so shall I.

NIETZ: Excellent! We must make arrangements! I'll go on ahead and sort everything out !

LOU   First I have some...business to conclude.

NIETZ: Of course, of course. - But this is wonderful news! We shall have such a summer, I promise you that.

LOU: I hope so.

NIETZ: I *know* so. Like-minds living together: what could be better? When can you come?

LOU: I don't know.

NIETZ: End of the week?

LOU: Really, at this moment, I couldn't say ---

NIETZ: Early next week? No of course not – forgive me! I'm jumping ahead of myself – of everybody.

The sound of Rée and Heinrich returning.

LOU: I should be going.

NIETZ: Really? So soon?

LOU: My chaperone: Heinrich and I gave her the slip, sort of: she's expecting us at 12 at the coffee house in the Corso degli Inglesi.

NIETZ: Don't go there, too many English.

LOU: I like the English.

NIETZ: So do I, but not together. They drink too much.

LOU: It's a coffee shop, Friedrich.

Enter Rée and Heinrich.

NIETZ: Yes, of course. Anyway, listen to me: I've known you for a second and already I'm bossing you about: runs in my family, I'm afraid.

REE: Yes, that and anti-Semitism – you should meet Fritz's sister!

NIETZ: You won't be able to avoid her. She's coming tomorrow – as I hope you will, Fräulein Salome ---

LOU: Lou.

NIETZ: Lou.

LOU: I should love to. Heinrich, we should get going! Herr Rée, Herr Nietzsche ---

NIETZ: Friedrich.

LOU: Friedrich… - Buongiorno. Allora: allo spirito d'amore in solitudine!

NIETZ: Yes… all'amore in solitudine! Arriverderla signorina…

Exit Salome and Heinrich. Nietzsche walks to the window and watches them go. He then returns downstage.

REE: Well? What's all this about love in solitude?

NIETZ: *(beat)* I flirted with her! I found myself flirting with her before I could stop myself! I mean, I could feel myself flirting, and I thought 'stop this, you idiot', but I couldn't – it was far too enjoyable!

REE: There: I told you! She has that effect: she draws you in.

NIETZ: And I had no control! 'Love in solitude' be damned: she tamed me – in twenty minutes!

REE: Fifteen actually!

NIETZ: But that in itself is an interesting experience, is it not: to be out of control, witness oneself in freefall, looking over the edge – and jumping - a happy suicide.

REE: Steady on, Fritz.

NIETZ: Why? Why should I deny it? All my instincts tell me: she's perfect. And she *is* lovely.

REE: I told you.

NIETZ: More than lovely! You were right... madness of course, but why shouldn't it work? Well, I can give you a thousand reasons right off the top of my head: there's her mother to start with. I mean, she says she has a bit of money, but what will her father think when she moves in with three men. No, it's madness – but it could work; it *will* work.

REE: You see! That's what I like about Lou.

NIETZ: What?

REE: Men start talking to themselves after just one visit.

NIETZ: You're right. I'm being absurd. Utterly absurd. What on earth's the matter with me?

REE: Ah, man is so made that he can resist sound argument, yet yield to a glance, et cetera, et cetera..

NIETZ: Yes, I *have* yielded – without even knowing my opponent…

REE: And that, my dear friend - is love.

NIETZ: Love? Or weakness?

REE: Not weakness: softness.

NIETZ: But survival demands hardness. Still, I confess something in me … *(Pause)* Why does it have to be a woman?

REE: Why does *what* have to be a woman?

NIETZ: That we love. Not that I love Miss Salome, of course; I'm not suggesting anything of the like; but why, where the purest form of love is concerned - and if sexual attraction can be dismissed ---

REE: *(laughing)* Which it can't.

NIETZ: Why does it have to be a woman? What is it that we find in a woman that we don't – can't find in a man? Why do we have to love a woman? What does she give us?

REE: A softness. Woman softens the world for us.

NIETZ: But can't we men do that for each other? Doesn't friendship soften the world?

REE: Not in the same way. Women…draw out our own softness - because they're vulnerable, physically at any rate.

NIETZ: So we only love that which is vulnerable?

REE: They make us gentle: - 'gentlemen'.

NIETZ: Gentle – the opposite of heroic…

REE: Not if we protect them with our lives!

NIETZ: Then we act only with a woman's weakness in mind. I don't believe…. I don't quite know…what to believe.

REE: You don't have to know, Fritz; just have faith.

NIETZ: Like a religious fanatic, you mean.

REE: A devotee of love. Even Socrates was married: don't forget that.

NIETZ: Much good it did him - or her.

REE: Characterful wench, so they say! Kept her end up, in argument, I mean, though they did have children too, it can be done: philosophers can be lovers!

NIETZ: And yet it was his muse who came to him on his deathbed: make more music, she said. Just think: as you lie dying you realise you've neglected something as vital as music – and for what? A life of logic and morals.

REE: Better late than never.

NIETZ: Maybe. Maybe not. But yes, it took nerve to admit it. Paradox is a sign of fruitfulness, don't you think? Logic is sterile.

REE: In the wrong hands.

NIETZ: To which it is somehow always mysteriously drawn!

REE: All the more reason to love, then.

NIETZ: Yes, what could be less logical! *(Beat)* Her eyes are her best quality, I'd say, wouldn't you?

REE: Yes, that and her nose and mouth and ---

NIETZ: Her mere presence quickens something in me.

REE: Your heart, Friedrich...

NIETZ: Why would it need quickening? Maybe I've been dead. Maybe I've been asleep for centuries... Listen to me! I sound like a fairy tale! I hardly know the girl! Absurd. But then how long does it

(Nietzsche cont.)

take to find yourself in deep sympathy with someone, to know you're in perfect step?

REE: A second: the time it takes to exchange a smile.

NIETZ: Yes... her laugh has a kind of music, don't you think? It rises and falls: if I were being pretentious ---

REE: Which you are ---

NIETZ: I'd say it was like, I don't know – a Chopin prelude. There I go again! I know I'm being absurd - is it absurd?

REE: Fritz, you're using the word 'absurd' rather a lot, which is a sure sign –

NIETZ: Of what?

REE: The onset of love - which *is* absurd – and profoundly real – at the same time.

NIETZ: It doesn't have to be absurd. It doesn't have to be... anyway, I can't believe you're even using the word 'love', Rée: what's got into you: I've just met a perfectly pleasant young woman with whom I've exchanged some interesting ideas --- ***(turns towards sound of Rée snoring)*** *- It isn't* a love affair: I don't want that, I won't have that. Romance is absurd.

REE: That word again.

NIETZ: Men and women *must* be able to come to some sort of accommodation without falling back on that nonsense! And even if I do sense I might be able to entertain a certain affection for this young woman, that doesn't make it a romance: I don't wish to possess her. *You* love her too: I don't mind about that: I'm not jealous. If it were just some silly love affair I'd be jealous. No, if this is some kind of love, then it's just the beginning. I mean it's obviously the beginning, we've only just met! But if we are in such sympathy so quickly, think where our..

REE: Love?

NIETZ: Yes; think where it may take us! I mean what point is there in---

REE: Love?

NIETZ: Love, if it doesn't transport us, carry us above ourselves? It *will* transport us.

REE: Love is its own justification: it doesn't need a purpose.

NIETZ: Of course it does. What are you suggesting: that we all sit round gawping at each other like adolescents?

REE: Why not? I look back on my adolescence with great fondness. I fell in love every week, and twice on Sundays.

NIETZ: Please be serious, Paul!

REE: But why? That's my point. Let's just enjoy this for a while. We've met a pair of wonderful young people who share our beliefs, our vision: let's sit back and - well, just laugh with the gods for a moment or two.

NIETZ: What if the gods are laughing *at* us? No, love must have a purpose: whatever it is or isn't - I'll give it a purpose if it kills me. Anyway, I can't just sit back, this is too important. We've got to make arrangements: to start with: a suitable place for us all to stay, a modus operandi ---

REE: 'Modus operandi?'

NIETZ: Some way to live which won't cause a scandal: this is a young woman's reputation we're dealing with here.

REE: Lou thrives on scandal: it's the air she breathes: it inspires her.

NIETZ: Then what will she do when she has none to sustain her, when she's in the mountains alone, with nothing but low spirits to keep her company? Why am I even pretending to know the girl? I *never* pretend: I hate pretence. This is all ridiculous. I must leave. I should've left a week ago. It's far too hot; my head is bad...

REE: Fritz, calm down for god's sake! Everything'll be all right. You're bound to have doubts; I do: this a big decision - for all of us. For Lou and Heinrich too.

NIETZ: Heinrich, poor Heinrich: I didn't even speak to him today – unpardonable. I was so entranced...

REE: He won't mind one bit: he knows how highly you think of him.

NIETZ: So highly I ignored him completely when a woman entered the room.

REE: Not just any woman.

NIETZ: No... not just any woman.... *(Beat)* There's something she's not telling us.

REE: I beg your pardon.

NIETZ: Lou. About herself, I mean. She told me it all had to be sorted out this week. She spoke with an urgency, a certain anxiety. I wonder... and yet she seems sincere...

REE: Fritz, I have to say you are doing a brilliant impersonation of a philosopher in love.

NIETZ: An infatuated fool, you mean. Anyway! Why not be infatuated: it's a new experience for me! Makes me feel light-headed. As intoxicants go I rather like it. And she's a young woman: she'd be boring if she told the truth all the time... feminine lies give our stolid masculine truth a certain savour, don't you think?

REE: Let's drink to it! To Lou: the savour of love –

NIETZ: The salt of our earth!

They both down glasses of water.

Rée, my friend, what have you done?

REE: What?

NIETZ: You've changed our lives, you fool. Whether we like it or not, things will never be the same. For that at least, I thank you with all my heart. Here! One more toast: to the devastating spirit of change!

REE: And her utterly damned disciples!

They drink again. Fade.

1.3

The next day, Nietzsche's room again. Lou slowly paces to and fro. Heinrich watches her.

LOU: What's keeping him? I can't stand being inside on a day like this!

HEIN: You have to tell him, you know.

She doesn't answer.

And Rée – both of them.

LOU: Tell them what?

HEIN: That your heart has a prior claim on it.

LOU: Really, you do use the most farcically antiquated language at times. *(Beat)* Anyway, how do you know my heart *does* have a prior claim on it, as you put it?

HEIN: Because we kissed yesterday.

LOU: That was yesterday.

HEIN: *And* the day before.

LOU: Yes and nearly got caught. It was stupid. You have no idea how vicious that chaperone can be.

HEIN: I couldn't help it: you're beautiful.

LOU: No I'm not. You're infatuated.

HEIN: And don't you love it! *(Beat)* You're sure about this. You know what your mother will say; my father too. They'll cut us off.

LOU: Won't be the first time.

HEIN: Or the last.

LOU: They'll get over it: a few angry letters followed by a spiteful silence, then mother will want a conciliatory meeting at which she'll be rude, I'll be vicious back; she'll storm out and it'll start all over again. Families thrive on a good vendetta now and again - relieves the boredom. They'll get over it.

HEIN: We'll have little or no money.

LOU: We'll be rich in other ways.

(Beat)

HEIN: I told you you'd like him.

LOU: I don't '*like*' him – well, I do; of course I do; it's just such a pallid word. He's unnerving. When he gets going: he looks at you as if he's examining you, holding your mind up to his light - like a prism. *(Beat)* He thinks we're all mirrors.

HEIN: And how women love mirrors!

LOU: Are men any less vain without them? *(Beat)*

HEIN: So! Safe to say you're drawn to our professor, then…

LOU: Yes, I'm drawn to him; I'm drawn to a lot of people, even you. Why do you ask?

HEIN: No particular reason. Just interested in initial impressions, I suppose.

LOU: Initial impressions are that he's everything you said he was.

HEIN: And the moustache?

LOU: What about it?

HEIN: Oh come on: it *is* a bit Junker - so Bavarian! Pompous! It doesn't put you off?

LOU: Off what, for god's sake?

HEIN: Makes him look so old-fashioned! People's appearances matter, don't pretend they don't.

LOU: I'm not marrying the man, Heinrich!

HEIN: I should hope not.

LOU: Not yet… Actually, I don't mind the moustache; yes, it's on the large side ---

HEIN: Large – it's a bloody Dachshund! I tease him about it – mercilessly! Funnily enough, he's always rather upset. Why're you looking at me like that? For god's sake don't start treating him like some sort of high priest, he'll hate that. Anyway it's good for him to be teased: I've bet Rée I can get him to shave it off.

LOU: Well, I think it lends him an air of distinction.

HEIN: Oh please don't tell me you've fallen for the older man syndrome.

LOU: Older men have more style.

HEIN: And less libido.

LOU: They're delightfully relaxed, if you must know. Young men are always clamouring for attention, like puppies. You don't want to be a lapdog, do you Heinrich; please tell me you don't.

HEIN: If it means ending up on your lap...*(Beat)* Ultimately it depends on the arrangements; the devil in the detail and all that. There's Friedrich's illness to consider, have you thought about?

LOU: No, not really. It's not serious *(beat)* – is it?

HEIN: Probably not. Who knows? He doesn't. Nor do the doctors. I'm just saying that he's not a well man, he'll need caring for from time to time. Well no doubt we'll all pitch in. I mean, if we're all going to live together: that's the thing, I suppose: what does that phrase actually mean: ' living together'?

LOU: Presumably we'll find out.

HEIN: You might be in for a surprise.

LOU: I hope so.

HEIN: You might find Friedrich... he can be very conservative. You might be shocked at some of his opinions.

LOU: He might be shocked by some of mine! I know my own mind, Heinrich; I'm not as innocent as you think.

HEIN: I never said you *were* innocent; you're the least innocent person I know!

LOU: I take that as a compliment – in the Nietzschean sense! I wouldn't want to be thought naïve. *(Beat)* - Like you.

HEIN: I'm not naïve! I *have* read Nietzsche, you know: I *do* understand the radical nature of his ideas, well, some of them. Look, I'm the one who's been meeting with him ---

LOU: Which is why I intend to visit Fritz ---

HEIN: Oh it's 'Fritz' already ---

LOU: --- as often as possible over the next few days – before we all head North, that is. Then, we shall see what happens.

HEIN: Oh we'll see all right. *(Beat)* Of course, you know why you really like older men?

LOU: No, do tell.

HEIN: Because you're scared of what younger ones represent.

LOU: Which is what, exactly?

HEIN: Passion. You can waltz with these old philosophers; but with a younger man you might have to surrender more of yourself.

LOU: Really.

HEIN: Really.

LOU: And here I take it you're referring to sexuality.

HEIN: More than that.

LOU: Sexual intercourse.

HEIN: What?

LOU: With you. *(Calmly, deliberately)* What we're really discussing here is me having sexual intercourse with you – which, as it happens, I'm not altogether opposed to in principle, just not yet.

HEIN: I'm not talking about sexual intercourse, as you put it. I thought we had more in common than mere gender.

LOU: There's nothing mere about gender, I assure you: it dictates everything.

HEIN: Now you're parroting Fritz.

LOU: Don't patronise me: I share his ideas; I had half of them myself before I even read him.

Pause.

HEIN: So you're not averse to it, then – as such?

LOU: Averse to what – "as such"?

HEIN: Making love.

LOU: Why would I be?

HEIN: Some women... the first time can be...

LOU: Who said it's the first time?

HEIN: What? So you're not...

LOU: *(Sardonic)* A virgin? No. Don't tell me you are.

HEIN: No. No, of course, not.

LOU: Virginity's an embarrassment. I got rid of mine as soon as I could... then I regretted it. Only for a moment! Strange that such an absurd act should assume so much importance in our lives, don't you think.

HEIN: Is it absurd?

LOU: Of course! All that ridiculous, repetitious thrusting: the man ramming his cock home like a stick in the breach of a cannon. Sex is nothing more than an act of human artillery.

HEIN: I beg your pardon.

LOU: Orgasm is a detonation of ecstasy! The only difference being that everyone dies in the explosion: the men who fire the cannon as well as the women it's aimed at.

HEIN: I never thought of it like that.

LOU: I bet there are a lot of things you never thought of, Heinrich.... *(Pause)* The little death, the French call it: 'le petit mort': the climax of love.... But, of course, after one dies, one rises again... ideally. *(She looks at Heinrich coquettishly)* in a manner of speaking...

Heinrich takes her in his arms. They kiss, then she pulls away.

LOU: For god's sake!

HEIN: What's wrong?

LOU: Nothing. Everything. I just don't feel like it. I told you I'm not ready.

HEIN: You could've fooled me.

LOU: Not difficult, I assure you.

HEIN: So when will you be ready?

LOU: Who knows. Maybe tomorrow. Maybe never.

HEIN: So why did you kiss me?

LOU: I kissed you because I like you, because I find you attractive. And because I like kissing.

HEIN: What - anyone, everyone?

LOU: No, only monied aristocrats who own half of Germany. Satisfied?

HEIN: No - but I might be if you kissed me again.

LOU: I don't want to kiss you now: you're boring me with banal questions. Young men are so predictable.

HEIN: Well I'm sorry if my conversational skills don't match the great philosopher's.

LOU: So am I. *(Beat)* Friedrich is a great man.

Pause.

HEIN: Look, I know Friedrich is a great man: I'm drawn to him as much as you are: his mind, ideas: - but there's more to life than thoughts.

LOU: Depends on their power - and where they take you.

HEIN: Well at the moment they're taking you to a primitive cabin in the Alps.

LOU: Sounds wonderful. I'm not afraid of being alone, unlike you.

HEIN: I'm not frightened of being alone – so long as you're not far away. Lou: listen to me - seriously... *(Beat)* - I want to marry you: will you marry me?

LOU: No of course I won't: don't be an idiot. Oh Heinrich, don't look so hurt. If I were going to marry anyone it'd be you. I'd be mad not to: what woman wouldn't? A handsome, aristocratic devil with a whole state named after him ---

HEIN: Half a state – it's *Schleswig*-Holstein... just to be accurate.

LOU: In fact, if you must know: I do love you – when you're not talking nonsense about love.

HEIN: You do love me...

LOU: But I don't want to get married.

HEIN: Maybe not now ---

LOU: Maybe not ever! There's so much to see, to experience! Look at you: twenty-five and all you want to do is settle down and have lots of baby aristocrats you can spoil - or neglect!

HEIN: I do not. We can have children later.

LOU: Oh, well, as long as you let me know when...

HEIN: You know what I mean.

LOU: Heinrich, if we're going into this… situation with Fritz and Paul we need to be free of any encumbrances.

HEIN: Free of responsibility.

LOU: Yes.

HEIN: Duty. Rules. Laws.

LOU: Yes, we need to be ---

HEIN: Like children.

LOU: No, not like children - free spirits, free from everything except our ideals, art, philosophy, new ideas, feelings.

HEIN: And the body?

LOU: Yes, the body too: Fritz believes a whole philosophy can originate in the body, the non-rational makes its own demands; he says the body is a sort of tragic mute that dictates by sign language ---

HEIN: Then be quiet.. and let it speak.

Draws her close and kisses her.

There. What does it say? Your body to my body.

LOU: Many things. *(He kisses her again)*

HEIN: Such as?

LOU: How pleasant it is to love.

HEIN: And be loved.

This time she takes the lead, kissing him.

LOU: Regardless of the consequences…

He starts to withdraw but she pulls him back.

(Lou cont.)

And the morality of those who are…

Kissing him passionately.

…scared of the direction the body heads off in……

She starts to unbutton his shirt, he stops her.

HEIN: Not here, not now..!

LOU: What's the matter: are you scared?

HEIN: No, of course not. But this is…public, for god's sake!

LOU: So you want to hide our love? Just a moment ago you were saying I should tell them!

HEIN: Yes, *tell* them; not *show* them! They could come back at any minute.

LOU: Let them. People love a good shock; Fritz says ---

HEIN: Fritz says, Fritz says ---

Enter Nietzsche and Rée.

NIETZ: What do I say?

HEIN: Ah Friedrich, we were just talking about the body's influence on the mind.

NIETZ: The body *isn't* just an influence on the mind – it *is* the mind - just in a form we're too ashamed to recognise. I blame St Paul, that Pharisaic old pervert with his ghastly panoply of bodily sins! I'm sorry we're so late: I sat on my damned glasses; had to get them fixed: ridiculous, eh, a philosopher who can't see straight.

REE: Never knew one who could!

NIETZ: Which doesn't of course stop us showing everyone else the way. Philosophers: to hell with them!

HEIN: Present company excepted.

NIETZ: No, me too: I'm just as bad; worse: I ought to know better. I *do* know better... and yet still I prattle on. No, to hell with me too! Look, Lou, Heinrich, we've got good news!

LOU: Fritz ---

NIETZ: There are two houses right next door to each other on the lake at Sils Maria, and they're available in a month's time. I have the papers right here! All we have to do is sign and they're ours.

LOU: I've told my mother.

NIETZ: Told her what?

LOU: About our arrangements.

NIETZ: Excellent!

LOU: She wasn't impressed.

NIETZ: Even better! We must flee while the going's good.

HEIN: Just like that.

LOU: Seriously, Friedrich; she's threatened to write to my father: he could stop my money - unless I promise to drop the idea immediately.

NIETZ: On what grounds?

LOU: The usual rubbish: no respectable man will have anything to do with me, et cetera, et cetera.

NIETZ: You don't *want* any respectable man to have anything to do with you: that's the whole point: to hell with respectable men!

HEIN: All the same ---

NIETZ: Anyway, aren't *we* respectable? Rée and I are professors: we're so respectable we can't walk straight: drunk with respectability, we are. And Heinrich: a Von Holstein, for pity's sake: the man owns the very ground we stand on!

HEIN: I think what Lou is trying to say ---

LOU: I can speak for myself, Heinrich! – What I'm saying is that if we are to proceed with our arrangement it is better to realise that it will have certain consequences – for all of us.

NIETZ: Life always has consequences – respectable ones are the worst of all.

HEIN: In this case, powerful consequences, Fritz.

NIETZ: All the better!

HEIN: And your professorship?

NIETZ: That old ball and chain - I was about to saw it off anyway. Have done with them all, I say. Cut our ties for good and all! Look, one word and I will reserve those houses for us: are we agreed?

HEIN: Hold on, Friedrich.

NIETZ: For what? Lou's respectable mother and her respectable men with their respectable life? Come on! For god's sake it's not as if we're robbing a bank.

LOU: That'll come later when I run out of money.

NIETZ: So be it. A life of crime, why not? I've always had a sneaking respect for criminals; at least they go their own way.

HEIN: - To prison.

NIETZ: We'll eat, drink and be merry - and write brilliant books – when we've nothing else to do…

 LOU: How will we live?

NIETZ: Rée will pay, won't you?

REE: Steady on.

NIETZ: Anyway, my pension won't dry up over night: I'm officially ill: the old devils wouldn't dare sack an invalid: I'd sue their sanctimonious professorial arses off.

HEIN: You wouldn't have a leg to stand on.

NIETZ: I don't need one. I'm floating in air with the sheer brilliance of our effrontery! Come on, let's sign - but only if we're all agreed... Lou – you mustn't feel forced, you don't feel forced, do you?

REE: My dear, Fritz, how *could* she?

HEIN: Well I think we should wait a little.

NIETZ: What for, for god's sake!

HEIN: And I know your sister would agree with me.

NIETZ: My sister, what's she got to do with it?

HEIN: Why don't we wait and see: she'll be here any minute.

NIETZ: What?

HEIN: I can see her down the street. Does she always wear black? Looks like she's in mourning.

NIETZ: She's been in mourning since the day she was born. Look, wait, be damned! It's nothing to do with my sister: nothing's anything to do with her unless I say it is - and I never do, I can assure you.

REE: Doesn't stop her interfering...

NIETZ: For god's sake, shall we sign or not?

LOU: I'll sign.

HEIN: Lou ---

LOU: I said I'll sign! *(She signs)*

REE: Me too. In for a penny ---

NIETZ: In for a shekel, that's my Rée! Heinrich? *(Rée signs, swiftly followed by Nietzsche)*

LOU: We'll never have another chance like this…

Heinrich deliberates, then takes the pen and signs.

NIETZ: Done! Signed, sealed ---

REE: But not yet delivered!

NIETZ: And that, my friend, is where we're going now. Come on, Rée; you're the guarantor for our rent.

REE: Why me?

NIETZ: You're Jewish, it's what you do.

REE: Ha ha.

NIETZ: We'll be back shortly. Don't worry I'll deal with my sister!

REE: By running away!

The two men exit, leaving Lou and Heinrich.

HEIN: This is crazy.

LOU: Let's hope so. *(Beat)*

HEIN: And you still haven't told them. If you won't, I will.

LOU: You will not.

HEIN: Don't you think they deserve to know?

LOU: Deserve to know what?

HEIN: That I intend to claim you as my wife.

LOU: I'm not a plot of land, Heinrich: I won't be claimed. For god's sake, I've told you: I'm not marrying anyone: you included.

HEIN: But you *will live* with three men.

LOU: Yes I will – three, four - a hundred! – *and* a cat and a dog, not to mention horses. The phrase is 'live with' Heinrich: as in 'share breakfast, lunch, dinner - a roof ---

HEIN: And a bed: you'll share that too, I suppose.

LOU: Oh don't be ridiculous. Actually, yes: you know what: I'll share my bed with them too, if the mood takes me.

HEIN: And presumably they think this is a suitable arrangement.

LOU: I don't know: I haven't asked them. Unlike you, I'm prepared to let certain things just happen.

HEIN: Such as?

LOU: Anything! I'm prepared to let anything happen, Heinrich. I haven't got any plans. I don't want any plans. I want to live.

HEIN: At the cost of your reputation.

LOU: At any cost! Don't you understand? We're not ordinary people; we don't do ordinary things...

HEIN: And we won't pay ordinary prices either!

LOU: I'll risk it! Heinrich, I know you're concerned for me, but I don't need you to be. I don't want you to be. I want to stand on my own two feet.

HEIN: And if you fall?

LOU: Then I fall. People who take risks must expect accidents.

HEIN: Well this is one waiting to happen, I can tell you.

LOU: But what if it doesn't? What if it turns out to be the most brilliant thing we ever did? What if we look back in thirty years, when we're old and respectable, and all the little Von Holsteins have left, and we can say 'do you remember that summer that seemed to go on forever? Walking by the lake at dusk, the moon on the water..?'

HEIN: So...we live life in order to gain distant memories...

LOU: No! To change everything, to see everything differently. I don't want a small, safe life, Heinrich. I'd rather die...

Enter Elizabeth.

ELIZ: Die? Who's talking of dying on such a lovely Mediterranean day? I take it I've missed Herr Nietzsche and the other?

LOU: Fritz and Paul, you mean: yes, they've just gone out to ---

HEIN: - Get some newspapers.

ELIZ: Newspapers? Herr Nietzsche has changed his habits! He hasn't bought a newspaper in five years.

HEIN: No, well there was a particular article he wished to read, a review of his book.

ELIZ: He didn't tell me: I usually read his reviews first, to sort out the vituperative rubbish from any intelligent thing that gets written accidentally.

LOU: Accidentally?

ELIZ: Those idiots are too stupid to understand his ideas let alone assess their worth. I tell my brother to go and live on a continent that would appreciate him. You are?

HEIN: I'm sorry: Heinrich von Holstein, at your service, gnädiges Frau. And this is ---

ELIZ: Yes, when one writes, thinks and feels in such a unique fashion, then I'm afraid one consigns oneself to society's margins. Most ears are closed to what he has to say even before they hear it, if you see what I mean. That's why I'm always telling him he should make a new start somewhere else, where people have fewer small-minded prejudices.

HEIN: He does talk of leaving Genoa fairly shortly.

ELIZ: Oh not just Italy – or Europe: a completely new continent. I hear especially good things of the new German community in the Americas. He always talks of travel: why doesn't he do it? Somewhere utterly different.

LOU: And yet I think he still loves Europe.

ELIZ: Europe is dead and buried; what's left has sold its soul to the Jews. Let them have it, I say. Then, when there's nothing left of ours to barter, they can sell their own grandchildren – and good riddance.

HEIN: Yes, well, I'm not sure I can agree with everything you say there Frau Nietzsche ---

ELIZ: Elizabeth, please. *(Beat)* Why not?

HEIN: Well, there's no evidence the Jews ---

ELIZ: The evidence is all around us! Who owns the banks? Jews! Who runs the newspapers? Jews! The clothes stores, the greengrocers, the booksellers and publishers? all Jews...

LOU: Proof, surely, of their virtues, Frau Nietzsche.

ELIZ: I'm sorry?

LOU: That they are, as a people, and inasmuch as one can generalise at all, of course, highly adaptable and inventive - I mean, they would have to be, a sort of master race, no? - To run all those things you say they run?

ELIZ: They *do* run them, and they run them for themselves alone.

LOU: Really? - And all the flourishing businesses they created that employ us, give us all a chance to make something of ourselves: shouldn't we actually be grateful to them, rather than sitting on our big fat German arses complaining? Yes! those lazy, good-for-nothing Jews: how dare they employ their talents in the service of the common good!

HEIN: Lou, I think ---

LOU: Nothing but filthy, stinking parasites living off the wealth they created and then spreading it around for the rest of us! No, hold on, they created it, so that means they can't be parasites: therefore *we* must be the parasites living off *their* wealth! You know what: I'm confused.

(Beat)

ELIZ: I don't believe we've met, Fräulein?

LOU: No, I don't believe we have, Frau Nietzsche. A pleasure, I assure you.

HEIN: Yes, well, Frau Nietzsche, it *has* been an absolute pleasure.

ELIZ: No, no, the pleasure's all mine: I've been wanting to meet the young lady who has set the salons talking – not for all the right reasons, of course; but then I'm sure there are many lies mixed in with the little truth that is spoken about you.

LOU: I couldn't care less what people say about me – especially the sort of people you mean.

ELIZ: Maybe not, Fräulein, but isn't it a little rash to be so utterly indifferent to opinion? The world may be wicked, but for that reason it can also be a very useful ally to keep on one's side.

LOU: Not for people like us.

ELIZ: People like us?

LOU: We don't need such allies; in fact, we declare war on them.

ELIZ: Fighting talk, Fräulein. Well, I wish you well in your war on the world. Some of us, however, must adopt a more measured approach. Fritz... Friedrich – my brother is an ambitious man ---

LOU: Fritz? Ambitious?

ELIZ: Where his work is concerned. We have high hopes ---

LOU: He's the least ambitious man I've ever known!

ELIZ: Then may I suggest you don't really know him. How could you in such a short time? Such a complex man...

LOU: I know him a damn sight better than you ever will.

HEIN: Lou, I think ---

LOU: Yes, of course he wants to be read, but do you really think he'd give up his professorship if he were even remotely ambitious? Oh, I'm sorry; of course, you didn't know... Yes, Fritz is leaving the university – forever. And he's leaving here... We all are!

ELIZ: Really.

LOU: Really.

ELIZ: Well, I *am* behind the news, as they say. But then perhaps this is not such old news? In fact, may I ask when this momentous decision was taken?

HEIN: This afternoon. Well, about half an hour ago actually.

ELIZ: As long as that? Then perhaps there is still time to debate the matter.

LOU: It's not open for debate. Fritz has gone to deliver the papers to the agent. We're moving to Sils Maria for the summer.

ELIZ: Ah yes, Sils: beautiful at this time of year! Friedrich and I have passed many an hour walking round the lake. Which quarter are you

(Eliz' cont.)

taking houses in – that is, I assume you are, at least, keeping up an appearance of living under separate roofs?

LOU: We shan't be keeping up any appearances: we are what we are.

ELIZ: Which is..?

LOU: Friends. And lovers.

HEIN: In the Platonic sense!

ELIZ: Of course, *(To Lou)* I take it you know Plato's hierarchy of love? It's in the Symposium.

LOU: Yes and it can stay there as far as I'm concerned: we're not interested in the *theory* of love.

ELIZ: No, of course not, you prefer the practice – however much of a slut it makes you appear.

HEIN: Really, Frau Nietzsche ---

ELIZ: Elizabeth.

HEIN: Elizabeth – I really think this discussion has gone too far. I can assure you we're all motivated by the highest ideals. We're friends, as Lou says; we merely wish to live in close proximity so that we can share the intimacy of our ideals on a daily basis.

ELIZ: Really.

HEIN: Yes! You yourself talked just now about starting afresh, setting up a new community: that's all we're doing.

ELIZ: *(To Lou)* And no doubt this is your idea.

LOU: It's not an idea, it's a passion – one we all share. So you'd better get used to it. Not that it matters whether you do or not, frankly.

ELIZ: Perhaps not. Then again, perhaps my brother is not entirely immune to the influence of a person who grew up with him, a sister who shared a whole childhood, the loss of a father, not to mention the weight of a young mother's grief? Or perhaps you just expect me never to see Friedrich again, is that it? Perhaps you think I'll just disappear overnight, I'm sure you'd like me to! *(Coolly)* Don't you understand? Friedrich is unique, you can't just claim him for yourself: he belongs to everyone.

LOU: I know that.

ELIZ: Then you'll also know he's extremely fragile. But then how could you really know? Have you nursed him through weeks of nausea; washed the sick off his clothes; watched over his delirium; have you dealt with money-lenders for him; defended him when they tried to throw him out?

LOU: No, of course not ---

ELIZ: Then show some humility!

Lou makes to leave.

LOU: This is ridiculous: I won't waste another second listening to this!

ELIZ: Friedrich's life hasn't begun with you, and it won't end with you; just because you choose to walk into his room one day doesn't change who he is - god knows, you'll walk out again just as quickly!

LOU: I will not!

ELIZ: You're leaving now: a few words of truth and ---

LOU: It's not the truth I object to, Frau Nietzsche; it's the mouth it's coming out of. Anyway, you'll excuse me, I have better things to do.

ELIZ: Yes, like ruining a brilliant man's reputation, his entire hopes of advancement – all the work he's done!

LOU: Nothing could ruin that! Except your interference. Are you coming, Heinrich?

She flounces out.

HEIN: Frau Nietzsche ---

ELIZ: Elizabeth.

HEIN: Elizabeth – I really am most awfully sorry this has happened.

ELIZ: Why? Some people are natural enemies: it's only honest to declare themselves as such, don't you think? Friedrich is very fond of honesty – wherever it may lead. Good day, Herr Von Holstein. We'll meet again, I'm sure.

He bows cursorily and follows Lou. Elizabeth goes slowly to the window and looks out, then notices that Nietzsche's lists are untidy on the wall. She starts to re-arrange them, even picks up a pen to correct them, when Nietzsche enters alone.

NIETZ: Heinrich, Lou! Oh…it's you.

ELIZ: Hallo Friedrich. Is everything all right; you look out of breath.

NIETZ: I've been running.

ELIZ: In this heat? Here, let me take your jacket. You need to cool down. - I've been sorting out your lists for you…I hope the order is correct? I made a couple of changes; I put the authors in order of their centuries again, and the laundry list is out of date.

NIETZ: Where are… my friends?

ELIZ: You've just missed them. The young woman seems nice - intelligent; a little hot-headed perhaps, but I like that. I'm sure she and I will get along just fine, once we get to know each other, given a bit of time and peace and quiet, and Sils Maria is nothing if not peaceful.

NIETZ: Elizabeth, I don't know what you're up to ---

ELIZ: Oh don't worry, I'll rent somewhere out of your way, doesn't mean I can't keep a sisterly eye on you. You still need looking after.

NIETZ: Elizabeth, once and for all ---

ELIZ: All right, all right; don't get cross. I'll leave you to yourself. Look: the evening sun's come round: I'll close these curtains for you.

She starts to close the curtains.

NIETZ: Leave them.

ELIZ: You'll regret it.

NIETZ: I regret a lot of things.

ELIZ: I'll say goodbye then. You *will* at least do me the favour of an 'au revoir' before you head North?

NIETZ: Of course.

ELIZ: Dear Fritz, for such a measured man you can be so impulsive. I'm sure it does your constitution no good..

NIETZ: Goodbye Elizabeth.

ELIZ: Goodbye Fritz. Take care of yourself. Keep out of that sunlight!

Exit Elizabeth. Nietzsche goes to the window, assures himself that she's gone, winces at the sunlight, then slowly closes the curtains. Fade. End of Act 1.

ACT 2. Sc. 1

Sils Maria. Nietzsche's sparsely furnished new rooms. A week later. Morning. Blackout. A fearful cry is heard. Lights on Elizabeth and Nietzsche. Having arrived before the others she is seated by Nietzsche, semi-dormant on his chaise. He lets out another cry and wakes.

NIETZ: Help me!

ELIZ: Fritz, it's all right, I'm here.

NIETZ: My head is…pounding. Are the curtains drawn?

ELIZ: Yes, I closed them when I came in.

NIETZ: I can still see some light – it's blinding me - please!

ELIZ: They're closed, Fritz: I promise you.

Nietzsche leans over the bedside and is sick. Eliz tends him.

NIETZ: --- Thank you - for coming, after all I said, I mean.

ELIZ: I told you you'd need me…

NIETZ: I can't think why this has happened. I ate all the right things, exercised. I should get up ---

ELIZ: *(Mopping his brow rhythmically)* Just – stay – still.

Pause.

NIETZ: Still so kind to me, I don't know why you bother.

ELIZ: Nor do I: you're a very lucky man to have such a wonderful sister.

NIETZ: Though you say so yourself. Don't worry, grandiosity runs in the family! *(He throws off the bed clothes.)*

ELIZ: Fritz –

NIETZ: I've got to get up! I promise you. I feel better: – just being awake. I can't sleep, and when I do, it's a curse.

(He downs a glass of water.)

ELIZ: You must relax.

Nietzsche goes to the piano and plays very simple notes.

NIETZ: Playing relaxes me.

ELIZ: If you're sure… - I love it when you play for me….

NIETZ: I play to please myself.

ELIZ: Of course. I'm just saying I find it very peaceful too….

Pause.

Do you remember the way papa used to play to mama before supper?

NIETZ: No, and nor do you: we were both too young.

ELIZ: Well, you certainly *have* recovered quickly…

NIETZ: I'm sorry. *(Beat)* Little Lizzy, how do we manage to argue so frequently?

ELIZ: Because you're my horrid brother and brothers always torment their sisters. Play some more for me.

NIETZ: I'd rather not, if you don't mind. *(He rises)*

ELIZ: Please yourself. But I really think you've missed your vocation, you know that?

NIETZ: I play like the amateur I am.

ELIZ: Nonsense. You've inherited father's talent; mama always said if he hadn't have been called to the church he'd have been a concert pianist.

NIETZ: Or a torturer.

ELIZ: Friedrich!

NIETZ: But why choose when the church enabled him to combine both talents! Tormenting his idiotic flock with fire and brimstone, and putting a smile on god's face into the bargain: what more could any decent sadist want?

ELIZ: Father was not a sadist.

NIETZ: All religious types are sadists: they just use words rather than whips. Or in father's case, both.

ELIZ: How can you say such things?

NIETZ: I can say them because I have personal experience of them, Elizabeth – or should I say my arse has.

ELIZ: If father beat you it was because you were a precocious little so-and-so!

NIETZ: Because I beat him in argument aged six, you mean: not difficult: he was utterly provincial.

ELIZ: He was a very good preacher!

NIETZ: How do you know? You were two when he died.

ELIZ: Mama always says ---

NIETZ: Mama, mama, mama – when will you learn to think for yourself, Elizabeth?

ELIZ: *(Beat)* I try. I don't have your mind, Fritz.

NIETZ: Lucky you.

ELIZ: Not everyone can reason the way you do: I'm not an intellectual.

NIETZ: Nor am I, for god's sake: I hate intellectuals!

ELIZ: You know what I mean: you can analyse anything, everything... *(Beat)* which makes it all the more strange that you can't see the mistake you're making with this girl...

Nietzsche begins to recoil.

I'm sorry but it's true, Fritz: yes, I know you don't care about your reputation, but you should care about your work: people just won't touch it if you carry on with this affair.

NIETZ: It is not an affair.

ELIZ: Then what is it?

NIETZ: Two people sharing the same aspirations, the same ideals: *friendship*, Elizabeth: look it up in the dictionary!

ELIZ: Yes, but it's not just two people, is it? It's four: three men and one very young woman with questionable motives.

NIETZ: Questionable motives? She's not a criminal. What is this, a cheap novelette?

ELIZ: Her morals *are* cheap.

NIETZ: Oh for god's sake, don't talk to me about morals: you haven't the first understanding of the word!

ELIZ: Then explain it to me! Because I certainly don't understand what *you* mean by it!

NIETZ: Perhaps I don't understand either. Maybe I've given up trying, Elizabeth; maybe for once I'm just enjoying the company of an intellectual equal who also happens to be an attractive young woman. Maybe that's all there is to it.

ELIZ: Then marry her.

NIETZ: What?

ELIZ: If she's your equal and you find her so attractive – marry her.

NIETZ: Don't be absurd.

ELIZ: What's absurd about it? Men marry women all the time - hadn't you heard?

NIETZ: Very funny.

ELIZ: On the contrary, if you're serious about this…friendship, why *not* make it official, consummate it? That's what men and women do, you know.

NIETZ: I don't want to make it official; it doesn't need to be made official; it is what it is…

ELIZ: Yes: a scandal about to explode in your face – and ours! Have you even thought what this will mean for the family?

NIETZ: What family?

ELIZ: Your mother – *our* mother, Fritz: the woman who gave birth to us; who still idolises you; god knows why, you pay her so little respect. And there's my reputation too: but I wouldn't expect you to pay any attention to the effect all of this has on me. Mere association with the name of a woman like Salome ---

NIETZ: Then disown me, Elizabeth; here's an idea: why not just treat me as if I were dead: believe me, I'll survive the loss.

Elizabeth gathers herself, bag, coat, etc.

ELIZ: Sometimes I don't think you know yourself at all, Friedrich - for all your philosophy! Well, I'll leave you to your friends… They're late, I see.

NIETZ: They were held up on the border; they'll be here tomorrow.

ELIZ: Didn't they say that yesterday? And the day before? *(Pause.)* Well, at least *someone* was here to look after you. Goodbye Friedrich…

Fade

2. 2

The sitting room. A day later. Lights up on Lou, Reé, Heinrich and Nietzsche. Rée is opening Champagne.

LOU: It's beautiful! Fritz, I love it!

She gives him an extravagant kiss on the cheek.

And how the room gets the sun! But your eyes..?

NIETZ: They're fine. I promise you: going through a good patch! There! *(He throws open the window)* I can take anything the old devil can throw at me!

HEIN: And how much are we paying for this luxury?

NIETZ: Heinrich, you're too young to sound stingy.

REE: Too much, that's how much!

NIETZ: Shylock.

Rée pours out champagne in each glass.

LOU: How long have we got it for?

NIETZ: The whole summer! Longer if we want.

LOU: I want it forever!

REE: Well that may be a little more difficult to arrange with the landlord. Cheers!

NIETZ: To the summer of summers!

ALL: Cheers! Salut! Nastrovje! Chin Chin!

LOU: I can't wait to sort it out – : we must get a beautiful 'throw' to cover that hideous old chest! And those curtains will have to go!

NIETZ: Consider it done. *(He pulls them off their rails.)*

HEIN: Fritz!

NIETZ: I was thinking of doing it earlier anyway.

REE: Can we eat? I'm starving! And freezing! I know it's summer but it was Alpine in that damned waiting-room, they kept us standing for an hour.

HEIN: Yes, I nearly punched that stupid official with the moustache! Fat, hairy monstrosity!

REE: What: the official or the moustache?

HEIN: Both.

NIETZ: Hang on: nothing wrong with moustaches.

HEIN: Oh I don't know..

LOU: Heinrich!

REE: Yes, Heinrich, what's wrong with Friedrich's moustache?

HEIN: What's right with it?

REE: Bit on the big side...

HEIN: Big? It's gargantuan!

NIETZ: I like it big; Bavarian style; small moustaches are for small men.

HEIN: Now you're just boasting. Your mind is as large as your moustache – that's what you're really telling people!

NIETZ: I never thought of it like that!

LOU: Well I like it! Listen to you, Heinrich, one glass of champagne and suddenly you're insulting Europe's greatest philosopher.

HEIN: Ah Friedrich doesn't mind, do you?

NIETZ: *(uncertainly)* No, of course not. *(To Rée)* Is it too big?

REE: My dear friend, of course it is!

NIETZ: Well why didn't you tell me! I've been wearing it like this for years.

REE: That's *why* I didn't tell you.

HEIN: He didn't want to hurt your feelings.

LOU: *You*, however, have no such scruples!

NIETZ: No, no, Heinrich's right: it *is* too big. *(To Rée)* I blame you!

REE: Me?

NIETZ: You're my best friend: you should've told me. Thank god for the honesty of the young: I'll shave it off.

LOU: No, don't!

NIETZ: Tomorrow: first thing! *(A Prussian click of the heels)* Heinrich I'm in your debt!

HEIN: Think nothing of it!

LOU: Exactly: ignore him! It's a wonderful moustache. Heinrich's just jealous.

HEIN: I am not!

LOU: - Because he can't grow one himself.

REE: Ah a beardless youth, eh?

LOU: Exactly.

REE: Damned handsome one though.

LOU: Without a thought in his head!

REE: But rich! Fine proposition for some young woman!

HEIN: Thank you.

REE: All that money and no sense!

LOU: True, that is attractive. I could marry him and have as many affairs as I liked, he'd be too stupid to notice – if the lack of a moustache is anything to go by.

HEIN: I'll grow one tonight just to spite you!

REE: And if you can't, you can borrow Friedrich's! Tomorrow, I mean when he shaves it off. What do you say, Friedrich: will you lend Heinrich your moustache?

NIETZ: On one condition.

REE: Which is?

NIETZ: He swears to be as honest as this for as long as our friendship lasts!

REE: Tall order.

NIETZ: Well it obviously is for you: look how long you've let me wander about with this ridiculous moustache! Heinrich, however, is a true friend: aren't you, Heinrich? So what do you say? Total honesty 'til death us do part?

HEIN: Done!

NIETZ: Then let's celebrate! I know just the place!

REE: Not that ghastly beer-cellar with the stuffed ape?

NIETZ: The very same! You'll love it, Lou; the food, I mean, not the ape! Come on! I'll hail a cab! – And later on a good mountain walk! I want to show you the Maloja Pass at sunset!

REE: How far? I know your walks!

NIETZ: A mile, possibly two.

REE: Or twenty.

Nietzsche ushers Lou out, both exit. Reé begins to follow, then turns to Heinrich.

Come on Heinrich: the philosopher calls!

Exit all but Heinrich.

HEIN: And we all come running.

Fade...

2.3

A mountain-side. A few hours later. Nietzsche stands gazing. Beside him is a picnic hamper. Lou reaches him slightly breathlessly.

LOU: Shouldn't we wait for the others?

NIETZ: This is it: one of the highest points in the Engadin!

LOU: *(Breathlessly)* Very good.

NIETZ: Good? It's more than good!

LOU: I mean your impression of the romantic hero.

NIETZ: What?

LOU: Gazing into Nature's abyss! – At the reflection of his own solitude. *(Beat)* Friedrich!

NIETZ: Yes?

LOU: Not you! Caspar David - the painter?

NIETZ: Ah, yes! That gaunt-looking ghost with his walking stick! Yes, I wondered if you'd get it! I modelled for him, you know.

LOU: *(Sarcastic)* Ha ha… - might as well be you actually. *(Pause)* It's breathtaking. *(Beat)* Mount Olympus!

NIETZ: The gods embrace. Almost feels like an invasion of privacy.

LOU: Perhaps we'll be destroyed for witnessing it.

NIETZ: Ah the poetess.

LOU: Hardly…

NIETZ: But you are!

LOU: I do write… a little – sometimes.

NIETZ: I know. Well, I assumed you did.

LOU: Would you like to hear something… only a small thing!

NIETZ: Please!

LOU: It's an absurd indulgence.

NIETZ: On the contrary, *you* indulge *me* by reading.

LOU: No, I can't remember it. I thought I could, but I can't.

NIETZ: Nonsense! - Begin. I'm all ears! You can't let me down now!

LOU: I'm afraid it poses more questions than answers.

NIETZ: The only poetry I can bear!

LOU: Hold on… - no, it's absurd ---

NIETZ: I insist!

LOU: I don't really have a title for it yet.

(Nietzsche looks down respectfully as she composes herself)

All lovers are spurned in the end;
If not by love's inconstancy, then by time,
Debilitating age, dispassionate death;
However hot the air in that first room,
Love, in colder beds takes its last breath.

Do we then live alone, reject all ties,
Retreat into a sanctum of indifference,
Inhabit a lonely monastery for one,
Inhale the chill of meditation's tomb,
Where never came impassioned sun?

Ah thus the heart becomes a living grave,
And I've known many who lit incense
There to choke within its airless dearth -
Then let me shun heaven, where virtues fume,
For fires of sin, a brilliant hell-on-earth!

Nietzsche doesn't move.

It's not finished really; I'm not happy with the last verse... I'm sorry ---

NIETZ: For what? - My dear Lou...

LOU: You like it..?

NIETZ: No I don't... I adore it.... I – how... how did you come to write such a thing? I mean, when...

LOU: After we first met.. - You talked about the power of silence, about being truly alone: that's when words come to me...with a kind of intensity, a sort of music. Normally everything else distracts: people, things, even sunlight outside the window. Writing's like being locked up in your own private midnight.

NIETZ: Yes! Deaf, blind – no light but imagination!

LOU: Utterly alone - and yet one is poor without that kind of silence, I think: one must embrace it to come into possession of oneself.

NIETZ: You see: I told you you were a poet. Such thoughts are the air one breathes. They come from a great height, and yet you're at home in them, without fear.

LOU: I didn't say that! I have great doubt ---

NIETZ: Ah, but that comes with the terrain. As a writer one seeks to rise above one's doubts; but mountain air is thin, deceptive; one can get lost. *(Beat)* Sometimes I look at myself in the mirror, and please don't think I'm asking for pity when I say this, but I look and I think who is this grey-eyed, hollow-cheeked creature staring back? Not me. Someone else, someone almost grotesque with mistrust and loneliness. A monster.

She sits with Nietzsche and takes his hand in hers.

LOU: Love can kill monsters.

NIETZ: In fairy tales, perhaps; even then not without a fight.

LOU: Or the pretence of one… you mention paintings: I saw a Uccello; the one in Florence where the dragon surrenders to St George – and he tames it without killing it.

NIETZ: Love conquers all…

LOU: And recreates us in its own likeness.

NIETZ: Watch out, young lady: you've created a new male god of love. Aphrodite will be jealous.

LOU: Let her be.

She gently kisses Nietzsche's hand. Silence.

Friedrich! Look: is that an eagle?

NIETZ: And another!

LOU: Three! *(Beat)* What must that feel like: to soar with no danger!

NIETZ: Why would you ever come down to earth? I tell you if I had their wings ---

LOU: Don't you? When you write?

NIETZ: *(contemptuously)* Not like that! *(Beat)* Writing's a flight of fancy – a refuge from real inspiration - well *my* writing, not yours: I do it because I've nothing better to do.

LOU: You don't mean that.

NIETZ: No *(beat)* I don't. Forgive my disingenuousness: it's a vice I've cultivated to divert fools who think I'm mad. I write…I write because I have no choice.

LOU: Because if you didn't write, you'd go mad.

NIETZ: No, the opposite, actually: I write expressly to *go* mad – to celebrate a certain kind of insanity. *(He pours out wine)* Here's to Dionysus! Defender of divine madness - without whose chaos there would be – could be – no art, love, music – nothing. There you are: if I write anything of any worth, Miss Salome, it's to celebrate the collision of chaos and desire! Everything else, logic, deduction, induction – nothing but rationalist nonsense! What good is that gazing into the abyss. The heart's depths, that's where inspiration comes from!

LOU: And its heights!

NIETZ: Exactly. Like lightning, with no division between the light and the landscape, between you and your thought. One moment there's nothing; the next: everything!

LOU: And who cares where it comes from!

NIETZ: Yes! So what if Christians want to call it God? That's their problem. It's here: inside you; you, but not you, greater than you: leading you on, and not always upwards. Down into the underworld. Orpheus!

LOU: Bringing us back from the dead.

NIETZ: Singing us back into being!

LOU: Because *only* song animates us!

NIETZ: *That's* what real thought is!

LOU: Then it's no different from poetry....

NIETZ: Yes, I confess! I'm a poet, not a philosopher.

LOU: Is there any difference?

NIETZ: Ha – checkmate! I suppose it comes down to one's choice of words.

LOU: Assuming, of course, that it's you who choose them *(Nietzsche looks at her, rapt)* - and not the other way round. Words, I mean: they predispose us to feel – in certain ways. Every word we use has been built up by thousands of years of ---

NIETZ: Wind and rain, the blood and tears of ancestors...

LOU: Yes...well, the idea of ancestors is old hat, these days ---

NIETZ: But that doesn't mean they don't watch over us, shed tears for us: haunt us in the words we use.

LOU: Yes: words like 'intimacy, enmity... grief... bereavement.

NIETZ: Exactly! Tell me: why *do* you write? You told me 'when' – but *why?*

LOU: To make things real. To become the things I see, feel. When I put the eagle into words, I become more like him...

NIETZ: Then, what does he tell you, your eagle? What's it like up there, feasting on perspective?

LOU: Ecstatic. There's nothing he can't see. He could describe heaven to us - but we don't look up. We look so small in the landscape of our lives....

NIETZ: Then I salute him *(beat)* and you.... Have mercy on us flightless birds....

Pause

That's the sacred... The eagle. His beauty. Alone in the mountains he loves – soaring in the height under his own power, taking everything in, nothing escaping his gaze, not the smallest prey, the largest peak; at liberty to swoop or glide forever – at perfect peace, accepting everything in his path – whatever comes - turning every wind to his spirit's advantage - everything making perfect sense.

*(**Beat. He addresses her without turning to her**)* Let me tell you a secret, Lou... more of a confession really... I have a fear... all the prose I've written: hundreds of thousands of words! Morality, religion...pedantry, nothing but secretarial emotions. Yes, maybe the truth needs an amanuensis at times – but then I hear your poetry... and I think - to hell with analysis! Let people do what they want, as long as it makes them like your eagle: crueller – sharper – imaginatively-speaking, of course.

LOU: I'll miss the philosopher. Men still need rules.

NIETZ: Maybe, but designed by the human equivalent of birds of prey – not sparrows! Acts of imagination! Not petty computations of reason. Reason doesn't improve man, it neuters him: he thinks that in reasoning away his spite he becomes better, but he merely becomes more tame – and less beautiful. Nothing beautiful comes to birth but through some form of violence against oneself. Eagles don't waste time reasoning!

Pause. As Nietzsche drinks, Lou still gazes skyward.

LOU: The third one must be their latest offspring. They pair for life. Don't you think that's strange? Two primitive creatures practicing that kind of fidelity?

NIETZ: Birds of a feather - beauty seeks out beauty. What *would* be strange is if, having found each other, they then abandoned each other. Anyway, is an eagle any more primitive than a philosopher struggling with a problem?

LOU: Problems *are* your element, Friedrich; you prey on them, like an eagle...

NIETZ: Or perhaps I'm their prey... - Like good old Prometheus, eh – pecked apart by my own problems. Listen. *(Beat)* Do you hear?

Pause.

LOU: What? I can't hear anything.

NIETZ: Exactly. *(Beat)* Nothing cradles the silence like a mountain. Nothing matters up here... All one needs is this kind of solitude.

LOU: And a friend – to share it.

NIETZ: Yes – friendship...

LOU: Love. *(Nietzsche suddenly rises)*

NIETZ: It's something in the air that does it, to be sure! The lack of oxygen: the altitude induces a kind of madness. I feel it every year I come back to the Alps. I mean Mont Blanc is not just a mountain; in fact it's not a mountain at all; it's an idea; to accommodate it mentally--

Lou now rises and moves towards him as he declaims.

LOU: Fritz...

NIETZ: - to make any sense of it at all one's mind must take on similar proportions. Why else do people like a view? Because it gives life a larger perspective.

LOU: Friedrich...

NIETZ: How else can one entertain the idea of a mountain; no, the reality of a mountain, without having a mind as large as a mountain?

LOU: And a heart as vast.

She kisses him.

NIETZ: Yes, one's emotions, the heart... absolutely..

LOU: One's feelings must flow.

Kisses him again.

NIETZ: Yes ---

LOU: Like a mountain river -

Kisses him again.

LOU: Coursing down the valley.

NIETZ: Undeniably...

LOU: - Back into the world of men.

Pause. They sit silently. She doesn't look at him.

Fritz... you didn't mind?

NIETZ: No. Why should I?

LOU: You seem distracted.

Nietzsche shakes his head in the negative.

I'm sorry – I should leave you to your thought ---

NIETZ: Anything but that... *(Beat)* We can come here as often as you like. Every day!

LOU: Morning, noon and night. *(Beat)* Listen: now I *can* hear something! Bells! *(She rises and wanders upstage)* Must be mass. Yes. Look: you can just make out the church spire from here. And the square! The lights are coming on. I swear I can see people!

NIETZ: No…

LOU: Yes, look: a little river of people flowing into the square. The town looks so sweet from up here.

NIETZ: Look at them: all going in the same direction: ants to a nest.

LOU: I know: let's go to the market!

NIETZ: What?

LOU: Tomorrow is Saturday- come on! From the sublime to the ridiculous. I'll take you!

NIETZ: You will not!

LOU: Why, is there something you're frightened of?

NIETZ: Yes, the human race.

LOU: *(Beat)* It's all right, Friedrich. I speak their language. I'll translate for you. Trust me: I'll protect you. Nothing can happen to you while you're with me.

She turns and starts to leave.

Come on – let's go down!

NIETZ: *(standing up)* Lou! Wait..!

Fade.

2.4

Sils Maria Market Square. The next day. The sound of market voices, a band playing, general hubbub. Lou, Nietzsche and Heinrich are seated at a café table. Their voices are slightly raised above the noise.

LOU: We've got ten minutes!

NIETZ: Until what?

HEIN: Our appointment.

NIETZ: What appointment?

HEIN: - with the future.

LOU: Don't tell him! *(To Nietzsche)* Just drink your coffee!

Behind Nietzsche someone almost makes him spill his coffee.

NIETZ: Excuse me! God almighty! Can't hear myself speak.

HEIN: Must be quite relaxing!

NIETZ: What?

HEIN: Not hearing yourself speak for once!

NIETZ: Why are they all shouting?

HEIN: It's a marketplace!

NIETZ: *(Shouting)* Yes but why do they have to shout!

HEIN: *(Shouting back)* To make themselves heard!

NIETZ: What's in this coffee?

HEIN: I put a slug of Schnapps in it!

LOU Heinrich!

HEIN: To warm him up!

NIETZ: I'm drunk.

LOU: See what you've done!

NIETZ: - with humanity! Look at them all: can't decide whether it's a farce or a tragedy. The good burghers of Sils Maria bartering their arses off! Look at Rée with that fat onion seller: she's enormous!

HEIN: You should see her onions.

NIETZ: He's buying them! Rée is buying onions!

LOU: Has he got any choice?

Pause.

LOU: Come on! One of you! Both of you! Up!

HEIN: What?

LOU: Dance!

HEIN: Absolutely not! *(Nietzsche smiling)*

LOU: Friedrich! *(He stares straight ahead still smiling)*

The gods dance with light feet; you said it yourself: I dare you!

HEIN: Don't be ridiculous, philosophers don't dance!

NIETZ: My dear Heinrich, that's *all* they do. *(Nietzsche rises.)*

(to Lou) You'll find me a poor waltzer. *(They take up a Waltz pose)*

LOU: Let's show these respectable people how to celebrate!

They get in step and begin to waltz round the stage giggling...

You're too modest Friedrich, you've done this before! *(to Heinrich)*

He's much better than you, Heinrich!

HEIN: Naturally.

NIETZ: I haven't danced since I was at college!

HEIN: Never seen anything so absurd.

NIETZ: Never *done* anything so absurd.

LOU: And therefore worthwhile!

NIETZ: Yes, stop being so sensible, Heinrich, it's bad for your health!

HEIN: Oh and you'd know all about that!

Nietzsche stops briefly, breathlessly...

NIETZ: Heinrich, anyone who didn't know you might suggest you were doing a very good impression of a spoilsport! Now come on...

He takes hold of Heinrich's shoulders and begins to pull him up.

I demand you cut in!

Nietzsche ushers Heinrich towards Lou, then sits down himself somewhat breathlessly. As Lou and Heinrich start to dance, Nietzsche occasionally claps in time.

Look at them! You should see their faces! Shocking!

LOU: Anyone'd think they'd never seen a dance before.

NIETZ: They haven't – not like this! Dionysians! Ah I feel.... What do I feel? I don't know. I just... feel!

As Nietzsche takes a slug of coffee it is evident that Lou's and Heinrich's dancing is becoming more ragged. Heinrich holds her closer than a waltz allows.

LOU: Heinrich, please ---

HEIN: It's a new step I learned.

LOU: *(deadpan)* Really.

HEIN: In Argentina last year – The 'Tango' they call it. The Creoles do it. First, you stay close to me ---

LOU: It's too fast!

HEIN: Nonsense, Then we separate…

LOU: I said it's too fast!

Using the dance's trajectory she breaks away; glaring at Heinrich she returns to the table. Heinrich looks up at someone across the market.

HEIN: Is that your sister?

NIETZ: Where?

HEIN: Over there: berating someone.

NIETZ: Probably found some poor Jewish stallholder to insult. Don't move: she can't see us from here….

LOU: Your sister, Friedrich: is she always so… on edge..?

NIETZ: Of course! She's a perfect member of the bourgeoisie: she simmers with good manners, positively boils over with them.

LOU: We noticed.

NIETZ: I tell her: stop being so damned virtuous! But the more prim and proper she is in public the more privately angry she becomes. Our upbringing, I'm afraid: with your father as parish priest what chance do you have? I was a terrible prig. I could recite my whole catechism in Latin at the age of four: imagine: disgusting! *(Laughs)* Mother loved it, of course. Until the tantrums began. Nobody knew why: I certainly didn't. One day I refused to recite some trite verse or other; tipped a tray of coffee over instead. Best thing I ever did. I knew at that point I'd hit on something vital – I don't mean rebellion, that's banal; not the power of irrationality either – but the power *behind* irrationality, *hidden in it!* - exploit that and you've got Dionysian energy on tap! - How much Schnapps did you put in this coffee..?

HEIN: She's coming over!

NIETZ: Christ, let's go!

LOU: You can't keep running away from your sister, Friedrich!

NIETZ: Why not? I've been doing it for thirty years!

HEIN: It's time for our appointment anyway, Lou: come on!

NIETZ: Which way?

LOU: It's just over there. Follow me!

They rise from the table and thread themselves through the crowd.

NIETZ: What about Rée?

HEIN: It's too late: the onion-seller's got him in a death-grip.

NIETZ: God, I detest crowds!

LOU: Which is why we're taking a diversion.

LOU: In here!

NIETZ: What? What on earth are we going in here for?

They pass through the doorway into a photographer's studio occupied by a large standing camera of the age, some chairs, odd props, costumes, military, etc; a mirror, and some rustic stuff, a wheel barrow, hoe, and a small wooden cart. The proprietor busies himself.

LOU: We need a record!

NIETZ: A record? What of? What sort of record?

HEIN: You'll see! Excuse me sir, we'd like to employ your expertise for a moment.

PROP: Certainly sir. Picture of all three of you? A nice group shot, as I call it?

NIETZ: No, no, no; count me out.

LOU: Fritz, don't be a spoilsport; you said we needed to celebrate being here; well here we are!

HEIN: Yes, come on Fritz, it'll only take a minute.

PROP: The young gentleman's right, sir: one minute to make a record for the whole of posterity! Don't be shy, sir; all over in a flash, sir, I promise you. A flash, you see: - my little joke.

NIETZ: *(protesting as they usher him in front of camera)* Oh really…

PROP: Now! If you'd all stand over here please! How would you like the group arranged? The lady seated in front of the two gentlemen?

NIETZ: Wait, what about a proper setting? Something more theatrical!

They both look at him surprised.

Well if we're going to make asses of ourselves let's at least do it with some panache!

PROP: That's the spirit sir!

NIETZ: I know! Let's go and get that ape from the café!

REE: What on earth for?

NIETZ: To show our support for Darwin! Man and ape: brothers in arms! Partners in crime!

HEIN: And where exactly does Lou fit in to this masculine paradise?

NIETZ: She doesn't! That's the point. In posing next to the ape we prove both how brilliant Darwin was - and how stupid. How could an ape have fathered our dear Lou? And even if he did, what does that say about his daughter's future? Yes, we've evolved – so what? The question is 'where are we clever beasts heading?' – Fetch the ape, I tell you!

PROP: Er, I'd rather you didn't – begging your pardon, sir.

NIETZ: Why not?

PROP: It might create a kerfuffle. I don't get on too well with the café owner, you see.

NIETZ: Shame…

PROP: I've got some costumes…

LOU: *(alarmed)* Costumes?

NIETZ: No, no. No costumes! We must be absolutely of the age! Modernity! That's what this machine is all about isn't it, this camera of yours? Then let's take a photograph of the age! One that sums up our culture, or lack of it, for posterity! Here, Lou, I see just the thing: step this way, my friends!

PROP: Ah I see sir is going for the pastoral image; an excellent choice, if I may say so.

NIETZ: Yes but with one or two radical amendments, I think! Heinrich, get in!

HEIN: What? In that old thing? You must be joking!

NIETZ: Of course I am! Now get in. Not you, Lou!

Heinrich and Nietzsche get in the cart without Lou.

PROP: Several clients have chosen precisely this property to stage a scene of rustic peace and harmony: a lovely choice, sir!

Heinrich and Nietzsche are still clambering in.

NIETZ: Precisely! Because harmony and peace is exactly what we're all *not* going to see in the coming decades! War, my friend: that's what we need! - If not an actual one, then a bloody war of ideas!

PROP: Is it?

NIETZ: As an antidote to the virus of bourgeois contentment. At least once a generation! Look around you sir: culture rots; we stink with the bacteria of boredom!

PROP: Do we?

NIETZ: Reek of it! *(Beat)* Fortunately the catharsis of war purges us… in some tragically necessary way. War between everything and everyone; prejudice against prejudice, men against women, youth against age: you and me both driven to the guillotine, that's what we'll depict, Heinrich! Lou, pick up that whip.

PROP: Well, the cart's certainly never been used in that spirit before.

LOU: That's because you've never had a philosopher in your studio.

Pause.

NIETZ: Hold on, this isn't working… No, no! We've got the whole thing the wrong way round! Come on Heinrich, get out; we need to assume our rightful place as beasts of burden! Lou, it's you who should be in the cart, not us!

LOU: Me?

Nietzsche and Heinrich start to clamber out again.

HEIN: For god's sake, let's sort it out one way or the other!

NIETZ: You should be driving us, Lou! First, it's total war between men; then a reversion to the opposite extreme: total dominance by woman, that's where we're heading!

PROP: We've already got it in my household!

NIETZ: Exactly! Slave and slave-driver! The cruel irony: the more mild-mannered men become, the more bovine their destiny. Gentle beasts driven by the cruel herdswoman of the female will. Take that, Mr Photographer!

PROP: If you say so sir. Hold still now...

NIETZ: Stop fidgeting, Heinrich, you're upsetting the entire balance of culture!

HEIN: You're standing on my foot.

NIETZ: Sorry.

PROP: Completely still, please, ladies and gentlemen!

Flash.

Fade.

2.5

A day later. Nietzsche's room. Nietzsche is fidgeting in a chair as Lou tries to trim his moustache.

LOU: Hold still, damn you – or my scissors will slip and I'll end up cutting off more than you bargained for!

NIETZ: What *did* I bargain for?

LOU: A cheap hair cut.

NIETZ: With a bit of emasculation thrown in.

LOU: Don't be absurd – I'm merely trimming a wild man's whiskers and turning him into a ---

NIETZ: Tame pussy cat.

LOU: Hold still!

NIETZ: You do realise this is biblical.

LOU: What is?

NIETZ: You shearing me like this – me allowing you to do it - deeply symbolic. Samson and all that.

LOU: Yes, well if you're too weak to get out of the chair when I've finished you'll know you've been had.

NIETZ: Perhaps it's already too late.

LOU: Meaning?

NIETZ: I'm already lost – in submitting to your will.

LOU: What will is that? You asked me to do this!

NIETZ: Not the moustache – *(beat)* I mean in making me confide in you.

LOU: Making you?

NIETZ: I can't stop myself telling you everything about myself – everything I think... believe! It's pathetic.

LOU: Why, in god's name?

NIETZ: One ought to keep something of oneself back – even from those one loves... in the way that you and I love each other, I mean.

LOU: And if one doesn't? – Keep something back?

NIETZ: One becomes weaker – dependent – vulnerable to the other person's faithlessness – treachery.

LOU: Is sir calling his barber a traitress?

NIETZ: Oh we all have a little of the vice in us, I don't doubt. Why shouldn't *you*?

LOU: I think you're the least grateful customer I've ever had.

NIETZ: I'm the *only* customer you've ever had!

LOU: You'll thank me when you see my work.

NIETZ: Samson was blinded by his love for Delilah. Perhaps I won't see anything ever again after loving you.

LOU: And all this from trimming a moustache.

NIETZ: Well, let's just say: there are biblical precedents.

LOU: And we all know how much store you set by the bible.

NIETZ: I do, actually. I love the Old Testament prophets – as poets, I mean. They wrote with great visionary power.

LOU: And pulled temples down when their hair was cut by faithless women!

NIETZ: That too.

She steps back to survey her work, then presents a mirror for Nietzsche to look in.

LOU: Et voilà! How does sir like his new style? Is it not à la mode?

NIETZ: Terribly. Henceforth I shall be unrecognisable – even to myself! You couldn't've done me a greater favour!

LOU: Fool…

NIETZ: Unquestionably… *(He takes and kisses her hand. Fade)*

2.6.

Nietzsche's room. Same day. Nietzsche stands at the window looking out. Rée sits watching him. The distant sound of Lou's laughter is heard through window.

NIETZ: I love the sound of her laughter! I can hardly believe I'm saying it, Rée, but I feel... renewed!

REE: I liked you as you were.

NIETZ: No, this is the new improved me, I assure you! Buy now whilst stocks last! There may never be another redeemed sinner like me! Life is sweet!

REE: Excuse me: is this Friedrich Nietzsche, renowned philosopher of nihilism and despair?

NIETZ: I'm not renowned – and I never proclaimed despair! I hate despair: despair is for poets - and modern novelists besotted with misery. No, today, there is very definitely hope for mankind! Even the worst of them! - What about that market, did you see that onion-seller!

REE: Very funny.

NIETZ: Ah, Poor Rée: what a fright! Never seen a plainer woman.

REE: Had to buy half a ton of onions just to get away from her.

NIETZ: Never mind, onion soup all round!

REE: Yes – and onion pie, and onion tart and baked onions, and boiled onions.

NIETZ: How is it women get us do things we don't want to do - before we even notice it!

REE: Like buying half a ton of onions, you mean.

NIETZ: Metaphorically-speaking, yes! – so that we end up saying, feeling – *being* the opposite of the person we thought we were?

REE: No doubt they prevail upon our better nature.

NIETZ: Assuming we have one... Did you see that detachment of soldiers in the square?

REE: Couldn't miss them; they marched straight through me.

NIETZ: But didn't they look splendid! Stupid, I know, but that brass band brought tears to my eyes; the more obvious the melody the more tragic it all is somehow. It goes right through you.

REE: - And out the other side. Ghastly bunch. The only good Prussian's a dead one.

NIETZ: Have you ever seen a dead soldier? They look like sculptures; works of art. Even the worst achieve a kind of pathos in death. I remember one I helped in '70, just weeks before the French surrender, a giant of a man – when I was in the ambulance corps. Well, I didn't help much; sat with him, as he died. A shell had shattered his skull. He couldn't say anything; just looked at me with death in his eyes – as if *I were* death – and died. I remember that stare though, as if he'd realised something too late. – *(Beat)* How we all stared at them yesterday! – in their Prussian blue uniforms, and us in our dull grey! - You want to know what the greatest danger of the age is?

REE: *(parroting)* Yes, I want to know what the greatest danger facing the age is.

NIETZ: A love of uniforms! A great lumpen mass of us: Capitalists, Socialists, anarchists marching to and fro! First to the left, then to the right - flattening the cultural landscape, spreading the plague of conformity! Nothing but blind followers *(Turns to Rée)* - Coffee?

REE: Only if you're having one?

NIETZ: Touché!

Nietzsche pours coffee. The sound of laughter through the window.

The young are happy.

REE: Indeed, our young fräulein is in clover, I think. Why shouldn't she be, surrounded by lovers?

NIETZ: Long may she continue to be.

REE: And long may love itself continue to be so uncomplicated!

NIETZ: What *should* complicate it?

REE: Oh I don't know. Nothing. Everything. Love has a way of finding complications. He *is* in love with her, you know.

NIETZ: Of course he is. You told me that the day we met.

REE: I mean 'really' in love with her.

NIETZ: Then we must be all the more careful not to get in the way.

Enter Heinrich.

HEIN: Am I disturbing you?

REE: No, no, I was just leaving. I'll catch up with you later Fritz… *(Exit)*

HEIN: *(To Nietzsche)* Are you sure?

NIETZ: Come in for god's sake! Put me out of my misery: my brain is more than usually stolid today!

HEIN: I wanted to speak to you – about something personal; something that affects us all, or could affect us all, in a manner of speaking.

NIETZ: Heinrich, I'm enthralled: what subject could possibly be so comprehensive? Apart from love, I suppose, and you know I'm no expert on that. But don't let that stop you: I mean, if it was love… I can always give the subject a try.

HEIN: No, no…well, yes – in a way…but it can wait - what are you writing – if you don't mind me asking?

NIETZ: The logic of suicide – if you don't mind me telling! I can't see any way of refuting it. Don't worry, I'm not about to shoot myself: I can't afford the gun. No, it's just something Socrates said to his doctor on his deathbed.

HEIN: Ah yes! 'I owe a ram to Asclepius..' – The ram being the payment one gave to one's doctor on being healed by his treatment.

NIETZ: Bravo! And life being the disease! So what do you think, Heinrich: is death our only cure?

HEIN: Not when we have the capacity to love.

NIETZ: True, Socrates couldn't stand his wife, they say.

HEIN: And pleasure outweighs pain – well it has in my life. Entirely selfish, I know; I've suffered no great illness or disease.

NIETZ: And you were born into an aristocratic family.

HEIN: Hardly my fault.

NIETZ: I didn't say it was. But what if a man suffers far more than he enjoys, what then? Wouldn't he be merely sensible to put an end to it? A man, say, who suffers some great loss: wife, child, fortune: a veritable Job of distress and affliction, with no prospect in sight but further deprivation: why should he endure it, why facilitate the phenomenon that enables such distress? Life: why bear it?

HEIN: Because things improve: happiness always returns: we must endure what we can't enjoy.

NIETZ: And overcome both! Exactly! The great soul doesn't go shopping in fate's marketplace like some fastidious bourgeois! We triumph over life by accepting everything it throws at us.

HEIN: Not everything ---

NIETZ: Whatever comes our way! It's pain that proves us, not pleasure; anyone can deal with pleasure, but getting to grips with pain,

(Nietzsche cont.)

wrestling *that* into submission: that's what strengthens the soul! – Why should life be only gain? Why should we give no value to loss? Our whole life is loss. *(Beat)* There aren't four seasons, there's one: autumn; we *are* autumn; thoughts, feelings: love, all of it fades - the moment it flourishes.

Pause

HEIN: So what point is there? To anything?

NIETZ: None – unless we choose to give loss a meaning!

HEIN: Forgive me, Friedrich, but loss is loss; pain is pain. All this, it's theory, not life. That's why I wanted to talk to you about ---

NIETZ: It *is* life! - …My life. And I accept it – more than that: embrace it! Otherwise it's all just a question of luck, a lottery; and no sane man could tolerate such a ludicrous proposition. No, you can't determine fate; but you can wring meaning from it: make it a prized possession: turn it to gold! What if you had *this* life, right now; again and again: the same joy, misery, right down to the last detail - could you really say 'yes' to that? Be careful now!

HEIN: I ---

NIETZ: Because if you *couldn't*; if you denied that prospect - that eternal recurrence - it would still mean you were picking and choosing, not willing to accept everything!

HEIN: I don't accept everything! *(Beat)* And nor do you… You go on about loss and pain, but you don't want them any more than the next man! That's why we're all here, isn't it – together? Why we're all in love with ---

NIETZ: *(coldly)* There's a difference between loving and being in love, Heinrich: one is real, the other is escapism.

HEIN: So what is coming here if not escaping? What is Lou if not a refuge from your loneliness?

NIETZ: A temporary shelter; when it comes down to it we're all destitute.

HEIN: Then why not be honest and live like a beggar?

NIETZ: I am a beggar: I just disguise it by wearing a suit.... *(pause)* - Forgive me... I'm supposed to be listening to you and all I've done is lecture you. What was it you wanted to tell me? You're in love with Lou – of course you are! I celebrate it!

HEIN: And she's in love with me.

NIETZ: I'm sure she is.

HEIN: And *only* me.

NIETZ: I don't doubt it for a moment!

Silence.

HEIN: Oh, well then, in that case ---

NIETZ: But do we need to be *in* love in order to experience love? Can't we just... love..?

HEIN: Maybe you should ask Lou that... *(Beat. He gazes towards the window and the sound of laughter between Lou and Rée)*

NIETZ: She's beautiful, I know; and not just in the way you mean.

HEIN: How do you know what way I mean it?

NIETZ: Heinrich, I may be half-blind but I can still read the look in a lover's eyes: you're in love, therefore you find our fräulein more and more beautiful.

HEIN: And you don't, because you're not.

NIETZ: I didn't say that! I *said* she's beautiful.

HEIN: Just not in the way I mean.

NIETZ: Yes, in the way you mean! But more than that. *(Beat)* Do you believe in beautiful souls, Heinrich?

HEIN: You know I do.

NIETZ: And the union of such souls?

HEIN: Yes.

NIETZ: Then you know what I mean.

HEIN: More than you realise, Friedrich… *(beat)* That thing I wanted to talk to you about…I need you to swear!

NIETZ: *(wry)* What, on the bible?

HEIN: Your word as a gentleman – that we can speak in utter confidence.

NIETZ: Why? Have you killed someone? I'm sorry, Heinrich, but you look so serious.

HEIN: I *am* serious. More serious than you are… - about Lou.

NIETZ: Ah, I see.

HEIN: I want an assurance.

NIETZ: About what?

HEIN: That your kind of love for Lou…will never change…into something that could….

NIETZ: Heinrich… I'm twice Lou's age. You and she were made for each other. My feelings are what they are: those of a confirmed bachelor. But that doesn't stop me loving the girl.

The sound of her laughter floats through the window again.

Who could resist such laughter? Or the woman behind it? *(beat)* You need have no fear of my love, Heinrich; it threatens me more than you.

Nietzsche sits down at his desk again, looks out of the window distractedly. Embarrassed, Heinrich retires.

Fade.

2.7.

A meadow. Later that day. Heinrich and Lou lie back in each other's arms. He reads aloud from a quarterly magazine.

HEIN: Listen to this one:

> "I love the dusty fatalistic scent of late Wisteria,
> Perfume of desire requited, fading fast;
> As if, more than love's own sweet hysteria,
> Lovers love the sleep that comes at last..."

LOU: Beautiful. Who is it?

HEIN: Ah – just some damn fool genius.

LOU: *Who?*

HEIN: Why do you want to know?

LOU: What do you mean 'why'?

HEIN: Why do you need to know who wrote it? Isn't the poem enough? It speaks for itself.

LOU: Well maybe *I'd* like to *speak* to the man who wrote it. Who knows: I might write him a poem myself - get him to fall in love with me.

HEIN: Then write to me...

She looks at him confused.

LOU: *(Beat)* ... You?

HEIN: I submit the occasional verse to rags like this.

LOU: You write poetry... *(He shrugs)* You never told me!

HEIN: You never asked.

LOU: But I *read you* poems, *my* poems.

HEIN: And I fell in love with you...

Pause. She takes the magazine and reads.

LOU: But it's beautiful!

HEIN: Don't sound so surprised.

LOU: Does Fritz know? He'd be so impressed. Sometimes I think he loves poetry more than philosophy.

HEIN: I don't care if he'd be impressed or not. I don't do everything to please Friedrich.

LOU: I'm not saying you do. *(Pause. Lou picks up the magazine and reads)* I can't believe you kept this from me.

HEIN: I'm showing it to you now, aren't I?

LOU: Not just this: the fact that you write – so... ethereally.

HEIN: I *am* ethereal. In fact, as ether goes, I'm the most rarified man you'll ever meet. You just choose not to see it.

LOU: Because you choose to hide it! *(Drops the magazine pointedly)*

HEIN: I don't flaunt the intimacy of my feelings in people's faces, if that's what you mean. I reserve them for...the proper occasion. *(He sees Lou is dismissive)* A poet shouldn't revel in his identity, it's vulgar; it puts people off. A poem should stand or fall by itself. Anyway, poetry isn't everything.

LOU: Isn't it? What else gives life meaning?

HEIN: Any number of things! Work. Family. Building a life together – what most people in the world do, in fact!

LOU: I'm not interested in *'most'* people; they couldn't care less about poetry or beauty. 'Most' people worship money, start wars; don't talk to me about 'most' people.

HEIN: We can't all be poets.

LOU: More's the pity.

A pause

HEIN: But they can be lovers. - Isn't love a kind of beauty? Aren't people beautiful when they love?

LOU: Of course.

HEIN: Yes! Because that's how it works, Lou! These words: 'poetry' 'beauty': they mean nothing outside what two people feel for each other. They don't affect the world. How could they? Love isn't abstract. It's private, personal; lovers fall in love with each *other*, write poetry about each *other*.

LOU: And then publish it for the world to read *(Picks up the magazine again)* 'I love the dusty fatalistic scent of late Wisteria...' Why did you publish that? Because you want people to know what love's like ---

HEIN: No - everyone loves differently!

LOU: --- That when you love, everything turns into poetry! Overflows into it! That's what Greek art is all about. You should hear Fritz on the subject ---

HEIN: Oh yes, that renowned lover! That oracle of love: we must consult him on everything!

Pause

LOU: Now you're sulking.

HEIN: I'm not sulking.

LOU: Yes you are.

HEIN: I just don't understand why you have to see everything through his eyes all the time.

LOU: I don't ---

HEIN: Then why do you filter every remark I make through his opinion?

(Pause)

I want us to be together... alone.

LOU: Heinrich ---

HEIN: Maybe it's selfish – love *is* selfish. If you can share someone you love, you don't love them enough!

LOU: So being in love stops us loving other people...

HEIN: No, of course not!

LOU: Then you don't mind me loving Fritz and Rée.

HEIN: No, I don't; just not in the same way - that you love me: with your body. - You haven't... *(Beat)* Tell me you haven't let him ---

LOU: I haven't let him anything!

(Beat)

HEIN: I thought for one catastrophic moment you ---

LOU: We kissed. – I kissed him.

HEIN: You kissed him... You let him kiss you.

LOU: I *wanted* to kiss him! *(Beat)* Oh don't look so shocked, Heinrich.

HEIN: How could you?

LOU: How could I? Well, you know, you lean forward ---

HEIN: Stop it Lou! *(Silence.)* ...When?

LOU: I don't know, last week, two weeks ago.

HEIN: Where?

LOU: I can't remember.

HEIN: Where! In your room, his?

LOU: On a mountain! We kissed on the summit of a mountain, with the whole world below us – it was the most romantic kiss in the world. There...! Satisfied?

Pause

I'm sorry. *(Pause)* I said I'm sorry ---

HEIN: I heard you ---

LOU: Not because I kissed him. – Because you're upset... and because you don't understand ---

HEIN: What don't I understand – that you're incapable of fidelity, that you're a liar! *(Beat)* – Well..? Aren't you going to say anything?

LOU: What do you want me to say?

HEIN: That you ... that you want to be with me, not him...

LOU: I *am* with you. Just because I kissed him doesn't mean ---

HEIN: For god's sake! *(Beat)* I know what we agreed - but it's different now; every time I see you... I can't bear the thought of him...

LOU: Friedrich doesn't want ---

HEIN: He must respect certain boundaries!

LOU: Set by you.

HEIN: By both of us.

LOU: I don't understand: why is the body more important than the soul?

HEIN: It's not but ---

LOU: Then why should it dictate who we share love with?

HEIN: You're twisting my words!

LOU: I'm trying to make things clearer! Heinrich, please, you're purposely misunderstanding me.

HEIN: I'm not. I'm just saying - I can't share you anymore…

LOU: *(Subdued)* You don't have to…

She kisses him.

HEIN: Then you'll let me tell him - that you won't… - that we're lovers.

LOU: Isn't it obvious?

HEIN: I want it made clear. Don't *you*?

LOU: If you say so.

HEIN: You're ashamed. You think the great philosopher will disapprove!

LOU: I'm not ashamed of anything!

HEIN: Then prove it: let me tell him!

LOU: Tell him what you like; for God's sake, tell everyone! *(Beat)*

HEIN: So you don't mind?

LOU: You really need my approval?

HEIN: Yes. I love you enough to ask your permission.

LOU: Then you have it... - but let *me* tell him...

HEIN: I want to come with you.

LOU: Why? Don't you trust me?

Fade.

2.8

Nietzsche's room. He is pacing up and down in his room in front of Rée who is distractedly reading a newspaper.

NIETZ: Philosophy is shit, I hate it, I'm giving it up! I'll take up something else – anything - farming! I've spent my life poring over books, squinting through a microscope – and all the time I missed the most important thing; spectacularly missed it!

REE: Wood for the trees, old man.

NIETZ: It's a disease! A predominance of reason in a man is always a symptom of impotence! Plato purports to use it as a tool for improvement; what he means is a device for castration!

REE: Painful.

NIETZ: And who wields the scalpel? The weak - who need to emasculate the strong – and all in the name of equality! Well let me tell you: there *is* no equality: the strong impose what they can; the weak endure what they must. That, my friend, is morality in a nutshell.

REE: Tough nut - for most people to crack, I mean.

NIETZ: Which is why they don't bother. *(Pointedly)* They'd rather just read newspapers.

REE: There's something about me in it actually.

NIETZ: All the more reason to ignore it.

REE: Don't pretend you don't read the reviews.

NIETZ: Only with a gun to my head.

REE: Bang! - There's one here about you, too.

NIETZ: Really? What does it say?

REE: *(Improvising a non-existent article)* It says your latest book contains strange notions...

NIETZ: True.

REE: - That, contrary to the rest of learned opinion, you believe society is going backwards in the name of going forwards ---

NIETZ: Agreed.

REE: - That you misunderstand the nature of the bond between men... and consequently suffer from a complete lack of fellow feeling. In short, you're an utter madman whose peculiar pathology is an absence of the faculty for love.

NIETZ: What? Show me that!

REE: - But that some parts of your book offer the hope of redemption, and even display symptoms of sympathy for - what's this? – women!

NIETZ: *(grabs the paper, realises there's nothing about him in it) -* Fool.

REE: What, me or you?

NIETZ: Both of us! Any man who believes what he reads! Life at first hand: that's all that counts. Philosophy is nothing – unless it increases your pulse-rate. – From now on I'm not interested in anything, any idea that can't be measured against the beat of a man's heart!

REE: - Which brings us neatly back to love… not to mention romance.

NIETZ: Romance! Romance is for fools with no will-power.

REE: Like us, you mean.

NIETZ: - And no sense of identity unless they're gawping into a girl's eyes. I never saw a woman I couldn't see through in five minutes, which isn't to say I don't find them beguiling…

REE: Ah the philosopher admits to a weakness!

NIETZ: I admit to nothing *but* weaknesses where women are concerned: that's why I've kept away from them.

REE: Until now.

Enter Lou.

LOU: Noisy in here today gentlemen….

REE: Nietzsche: he's disturbing the peace again.

NIETZ: Only because I possess none of my own. Distract us from our poverty of mind, Lou.

REE: Yes, what have you to say for yourself.

LOU: Nothing much.

NIETZ: Cordelia!

REE: Nothing will come of nothing: think again.

NIETZ: It's not ' think', it's 'speak'! Anyway, don't! We're sick of thinking. Let's go for a walk by the lake!

REE: Where we can all think more clearly.

NIETZ: Ignore him.

REE: Yes, please do! You're welcome to Fritz this morning; he's in a foul mood: he's given up philosophy.

LOU: What?

REE: Or has it given him up? I can't remember. Fritz'll tell you.

As they gather themselves to go, Heinrich enters.

NIETZ: We're going to the lake, come with us, Heinrich.

HEIN: I'd rather not... if you don't mind. *(Beat)* I have something to say. Unless Lou has already said it.. but I see she hasn't...

LOU: Heinrich....

HEIN: Though we both know it must be said at some stage.

LOU: Please...

HEIN: *(almost deadpan)* Fraulein Lou Andreas Salome: I want you to be my wife.

LOU: *(Beat)* I'm sorry *(coldly)* I can't imagine what's got into him.

NIETZ: My dear Lou, *you* have; into Heinrich *and* Paul *and* me; into all three of us. And we don't mind, do we gentlemen?

REE: No, in fact we're absolutely delighted.

NIETZ: The question is, do you? The weight of three men's love is an awful lot to bear.

HEIN: Friedrich --- !

NIETZ: I mean, Lou: can you shoulder the burden?

HEIN: Love is not a burden.

NIETZ: Then why is it weighing us all down?

HEIN: It's not weighing me down at all.

REE: You do seem downcast, my friend...

HEIN: I'm not downcast! I'm... - I merely wish to be honest.

REE: Well we all want that!

HEIN: Do we? Really? Or is this just a pretence? This, friendship! This ménage! I'm sorry, Lou, I can't help it. I can't bear it any longer.

REE: Bear what?

HEIN: All this talk, this theorising about love: you don't understand her at all! You're deliberately confusing her!

LOU: Heinrich, I *am* in the room!

HEIN: I must say what's on my mind! And in my heart...

NIETZ: Heinrich, no-one's stopping you.

HEIN: Yes you are; you all are, you tie everything up in words until none of us can move! *(Beat, turns to Lou)* I love you... – and I won't share you. *(Beat)* I want to leave. Us. To leave.

Silence. Exit Heinrich.

REE: Heinrich!

He glances at the others and exits to go after Heinrich.

LOU: I must go and talk to him. *(Starts to exit, turns)* I'm sorry.

NIETZ: For what? Heinrich being sensible enough to fall in love with you?

LOU: For the way it's come out... I wanted to tell you.

NIETZ: What's it got to do with me?

LOU: Things have changed.

NIETZ: Then we must change with them.

LOU: You don't mind... that Heinrich wants to marry me.

NIETZ: Imprison you, you mean.

LOU: Well, I don't believe that's exactly the way he put it.

NIETZ: All the marriages I've seen amount to a prison sentence – with hard labour!

LOU: A slightly jaundiced view of marriage ---

NIETZ: Is there another one? Don't do it, Lou. Yes, be in love with Heinrich – but don't marry him; not because he isn't a fine fellow; he is: the best – but because marriage... marriage is not for free spirits.

LOU: How do you know, you've never tried it.

NIETZ: I've never tried Prussic Acid either! Look, forgive my facetiousness. But I have an innate suspicion of any institution that requires the fear of God to enforce it. Look around you: how many happy marriages do you see? The young see the prisons their parents inhabit; and then leap into their own! Then they notice the walls - and can't remember where they left the key - or if they ever was one. *(Beat)*

LOU: So what *should* lovers do?

NIETZ Guard their freedom – jealously! Not sign their whole lives away for a few moments of...what? Bodily pleasure, blind sensation. Look, those who must marry - *go ahead!*- have children, run a business, vote, join the parish council for all I care! But not you! Not me, Rée – we're different, our needs are different.

LOU: And Heinrich?

NIETZ: He'll change. Truth is temperamental, it ages: when you're young it surges in the blood... I'm forty - nearly: the older you get: - rivers deepen, widen, flow more slowly.

LOU: I don't want to lose him.

NIETZ: Why should you, you're lovers: why should that change? Apart from all the usual reasons... Look, if it's security you want, you already have it.

LOU: A rented house - for the summer. *(Beat)*, Friedrich, it's beautiful here...peaceful: the river, the lake... but I'm not old. I don't want to be safe...

NIETZ: So you're willing to lose everything we have here!

LOU: What *do* we have? Hardly enough to pay next month's rent. Heinrich has ---

NIETZ: Money!

LOU: Not just money.

NIETZ: What then? Oh yes, a bit of land too; a lot of land – and status, women like that.

LOU: He has a future!

NIETZ: A future? I see. Strange, I thought I had one of those myself.

LOU: Yes, of course you do ---

NIETZ: But not the same kind as Heinrich – or you, it would seem. And there I was thinking we all had so much in common --

LOU: - And if I want children?

NIETZ: Children?

LOU: Why not?

Nietzsche rolls his eyes heavenward.

NIETZ: Children…

LOU: Small human beings, Friedrich: they come out of a woman's body - learn to walk, talk – demand things! - Children.

NIETZ: Yes, yes… I just hadn't pictured… you…

LOU: My own family. *(Beat)* - What then?

NIETZ: Then? *(Beat)* Well then we'd look after them!

LOU: Oh of course: simple..

NIETZ: All of us! We'd take turns.

LOU: Parenthood is not a game, Fritz.

NIETZ: Oh I don't know, it looks pretty daft to me! Oh Lou, I'm sorry: I *am* facetious. But actually I mean it: why shouldn't we all look after them? You, me, Rée – and Heinrich – well, *he'd* be their father…. *(Beat)* And so would I.

Pause. He sits next to her and takes her hand.

Just a different kind. There are different kinds of intimacy. Can't two souls fall in love; doesn't *that* have its own ecstasy?

Pause.

LOU: And the physical side: for you….

NIETZ: That… would assume its rightful place - in time; in a relationship such as ours, I mean.

LOU: And what is its rightful place – "in a relationship such as ours?"

NIETZ Whatever the two people in it deem it to be.

LOU: The two lovers...

NIETZ Yes… the two lovers….

She refuses to let him off the hook.

LOU: And what is that - for *you*, Friedrich - as a lover..?

NIETZ I… I don't know…. I've never been a lover. I have loved… a woman. The physical act… I have….

LOU: But not with someone you loved.

NIETZ: I imagine it would be different. *(Beat)* I'm not sure one should be… should allow oneself to be overpowered by the body; to surrender to it.

LOU: Surrender *is* ecstasy.

NIETZ: For women! *(Beat)* To submit to anything is to be dictated to by it; to be subservient to anything – even one's own sense of ecstasy – is a defeat.

LOU: Defeat?

NIETZ: For the will…. The will, the power of one's will is paramount. The man who cannot bend his own life to his will achieves nothing….

(Heavy pause)

Look, my dearest Lou: even if there were no physical side I would still…. Heinrich would be your lover and I… I would just love you…

Pause.

LOU: And what if this arrangement.. what if it were too much for Heinrich? *(Beat)* And not enough for me?

NIETZ: I'm sorry. I've said too much. I didn't mean to…compromise you. *(He lets go of her hand)* I just want… I couldn't bear it if anything came in the way of our honest communication.

LOU: Why should it?

NIETZ: The body, physical love weaves its own spell. Lovers sleep after love, don't they? *(Beat)* Not that I'm suggesting; I didn't mean to imply---

LOU: Fritz, stop treating me like a girl; I'm not embarrassed.

NIETZ: No, of course not. I merely meant to say that physical love can get in the way if two people wish...

LOU: Wish what?

NIETZ: Wish nothing to intercede between them and the pursuit, the ecstatic pursuit of truth...- whatever that may be perceived to be --- I'm sorry, I'm sounding like an idiot. What I mean is that the basis of real friendship - love - must be a mutual contract in which personality is subordinate to the pursuit of the truth – wherever the source of that mysterious essence is discovered to lie...

They both laugh. Pause.

NIETZ: All I mean, Lou, is that whatever arrangement suits you best, then that is what we should adopt. You should continue to *love* Heinrich – *not marry him*. And then, in turn, I, too, would be prepared – am prepared, to commit myself to... looking after you.

LOU: 'Looking after me'?

NIETZ: In any way that provides for our needs – *your* needs.... if the occasion arose. What I mean is, should our association require the protection of some sort of official recognition - only in the world's eyes, not ours - then I want you to know that I'm prepared to...

NIETZ: Friedrich, are you asking me to marry you?

NIETZ: No! Of course not! Unless you want me to, I mean: for the sake of ---

LOU: Propriety?

NIETZ: No, not propriety: protection – from the world.

LOU: I don't need protection, Friedrich.

NIETZ: You don't know: the world can be vicious.

LOU: So can I. *(Beat)*

NIETZ: All I'm saying is… ideals must be realistic; practical even! Paradise doesn't exist. This time we've been given together: it'll never come again…

LOU: We'll always be friends!

NIETZ: Don't say that. *(Beat)* Lou, intimacy such as ours… *(Beat)* You know, when I was fortunate enough to make Wagner's acquaintance - before the whole absurd circus got going! *(Suddenly moved by the memory)* - I used to stay with them, him and Cosima at Tribschen – before he married her, the scandal was intoxicating! Those weekends: the three of us, talking into the night, playing music, lunch overlooking the lake - he kept a wonderful cellar, the old devil! But that's just it: the wine runs out… After they got married, well, the usual, sterile propriety that comes with marriage crept into the old man: friends become enemies overnight.

LOU: Human, all too human…

NIETZ: *(Wry)* Yes!

LOU: You forget: I read your books ---

NIETZ: Then you'll know how inconsistent I am! Inconsistent enough to want this to last. Look, what I'm trying to say is it doesn't matter who marries you!

LOU: Oh well that's a relief!

NIETZ: What matters is our love!

Pause.

LOU: And Heinrich?

NIETZ: All Heinrich sees is the object of his desire: he has no perspective at all!

LOU: Then I'll restore it... *(Beat)* If I marry Heinrich – *if...* then he'll have to learn to see me better – with all my flaws.

NIETZ: And will he still love you – unconditionally *(beat)* ...as I do?

LOU: We'll find out.

NIETZ: In a loveless prison.

LOU: Then you'll rescue me...

Fade.

Music.

2.8

The study. Later that evening. Heinrich sits with his feet on the table, gazing at a revolver on the table. Lou enters. She doesn't see the gun.

LOU: Ah Heinrich... here you are! I've been looking for you.

HEIN: So here I am...

LOU: Why are you sitting in the dark?

HEIN: I can see better.

LOU: What, like a cat - *(she approaches him)* Lying in wait...

HEIN: Yes.

She drapes her arms round his neck.

LOU: For its next victim… *(she sees the gun and draws back)* What's that?

Heinrich leans forward on the table and gazes at the gun.

HEIN: That? It's a Gasser. Model 1870 - Double action revolver: cocks the hammer, strikes the cartridge, then revolves the cylinder – all in one click. Clever, eh? I bought it off a cavalryman the other day - in the market, as it happens.

LOU: *(Cold)* Why?

HEIN: Friedrich was talking about suicide – only academically of course. But I wanted to see what it felt like… to have the power of death in one's hands – literally…not theoretically.

He picks it up.

So simple really. One moment you're here, with all your desires and delusions… *(He points it at his head)* - the next ---

LOU: Stop it!

HEIN: What?

LOU: Don't play games, Heinrich.

HEIN: Why not? I thought you liked them. You're so good at them, after all.

LOU: Put it down.

Pause.

HEIN: Friedrich may discuss the logic of suicide *(beat)* but I could actually do it. That's the difference between us. Well, one of them! I mean, he's a brilliant thinker: Friedrich never gets tired of thinking: he can think himself out of any problem, love, death, suicide; whereas I think myself *into* them. I get tired of thinking *(beat)* then I want to *do* something – anything! Character is defined by action: that's what the Greeks said; and Friedrich loves the Greeks. Only sometimes I wonder

(Heinrich cont.)

if he practices what he preaches. I mean, to be human is to want to *feel* things as well as think them, isn't it? Feel them with your body – not just turn them over in your mind! I think there's something wrong with people who think too much: analysing things out of existence, until nothing is real. This...

He picks up the revolver again.

This is opposite of thought: the soul of metal: cold, indifferent to whichever hand wields it: not even Friedrich could bend this to his will... I could do it, you know.

LOU: Heinrich, please ---

HEIN: If I couldn't have you. I'll prove it – if you want me to.

LOU: For god's sake put it down!

HEIN: You don't believe me?

LOU: All right: go on then - probably doesn't have any bullets –

Heinrich points the revolver at his head and pulls the trigger. As the revolver clicks, Lou recoils in horror. Then, very softly, ironically, and distinctly, whilst staring at her, Heinrich says the word...

HEIN: Bang...

LOU: You bastard. You...

She tries to hit him but he holds her.

Let me go!

HEIN: All right, for god's sake, I didn't mean to ---

LOU: I said – *(wrestles herself free)* I... You .... *(beat)*

She slaps him. He tries to grasp her again.

HEIN: Lou ---

LOU: Don't touch me! *(Beat)* How dare you. Do you really think ---

HEIN: I don't think! I told you: I'm sick of thinking. – And so is Friedrich, he just can't admit it. He wants you just as much as I do.

LOU: That's not true!

HEIN: Of course it is!

LOU: There are other kinds of love!

HEIN: Not between men and women!

LOU: Maybe not for you.

HEIN: For any man! He's not a saint, for Christ's sake! What about *his* needs, *his* appetites: he must have some, or is he completely abnormal?

LOU: That's a cheap remark – even for you.

HEIN: Is it? Makes sense to me – one of the few things that does!

LOU: So don't live with a philosopher.

HEIN: What's that supposed to mean?

LOU: Certainties have a way of dissolving.

Pause.

HEIN: And love, does that dissolve?

LOU: I don't know. *(Beat)* You *know* I love you.

HEIN: Prove it: be my wife.

LOU: Or you'll shoot yourself…

He picks up the revolver and gives it to her.

HEIN: Yes, and haunt you to your dying day. Take it. Get rid of it. *(Pause)* You *will* speak to him.

LOU: Yes ---

HEIN: Promise me you won't let him argue you out of it. Philosophy's for books: love…is in here…

Touching his heart, he kisses her again. Beat.

I'm leaving tomorrow. There's a train. I'll wait for you. But I will be on it.

He exits. Fade.

2.9

Nietzsche's room the next day. Elizabeth is tidying again. Enter Lou who is surprised by her.

LOU: Frau Nietzsche, I hadn't heard you were coming.

ELIZ: No, my apologies; only I thought it better not to postpone a visit any longer: I plan to return to Germany at the end of the week, and Friedrich…my brother has a way of making himself unavailable when you want him, as I'm sure you've discovered.

LOU: No, actually Friedrich is always here when I need him. - May I ask what you're doing?

Elizabeth is neatly placing a crucifix back above Nietzsche's bed.

ELIZ: I trust you don't mind…. I found it hidden away in the draw.

LOU: Fritz hates crucifixes!

ELIZ: No doubt they prick his conscience.

LOU: His conscience doesn't need pricking – *(aside)* though I can think of something that does…

ELIZ: I know you don't follow the faith yourself, Fräulein, but both my mother and I earnestly hope; actually we *know* Friedrich will return to the fold one day; his father, our father, was a religious man, and so is his son at heart. As such, any little reminder cannot but help the cause, if you see what I mean.

LOU: The cause being his redemption.

ELIZ: Exactly.

LOU: By a funny little man nailed to a piece of wood.

ELIZ: You wouldn't expect me to dignify that with a response.

LOU: No, and you wouldn't expect me to dignify your grotesque little totem with anything but contempt. Why isn't he naked, by the way? I mean, have you ever thought? Your Jesus, I mean.

ELIZ: I beg your pardon?

She wanders over and looks casually at the crucifix.

LOU: Well, there he is, hung up bleeding to death, – but of course he's still got his pants on. Why is that, actually?

ELIZ: If that is a serious question – which I doubt – may I suggest that it has to do with modesty, Fräulein; a foreign concept to you, no doubt.

LOU: Not modesty: 'shame'! How you Christians love your guilt. Torture? Murder? We can look at that all day long, but for god's sake cover his penis! Sexuality, that's what really terrifies. Bodily pleasure: making love: you can't even say it, let alone do it.

ELIZ: Miss Salome, can it be that you expect me to be shocked?

LOU: I don't expect anything from you; I don't *want* anything from you. And nor does Friedrich.

ELIZ: And Friedrich, maybe there's something you wouldn't want from him either.

LOU: *(coldly contemptuous)* What are you talking about?

ELIZ: No, forgive me: one ought not be enigmatic over something so intimate. It's wrong of me even to broach the subject. Perhaps you and I might conceal our mutual contempt, temporarily of course, if only for the purpose of, well, plain practicality. My point is, Fräulein Salome – how curious you should have that particular biblical name by the way; anyway, what I'm saying is… *(beat)* - what *were* we talking about? There, you see, our hot-tempers have quite confused me.

LOU: *(coldly)* The fact that god is dead. - Your god.

ELIZ: Oh that. Huh. Fritz's atheism is, like so many of his extreme expressions, a necessary pretence to get him noticed. I'm sure he feels the need to do it, but equally I have no doubt that his intellect will, in time, grow out of it.

LOU: He's not a child, Frau Nietzsche; I'm sure you wish he still were! That's what frightens you, isn't it? That's all you've got: a spinster married to the memory of a little brother. 'Spinster…' how like the word spider that is: but then you do sort of lie in wait, don't you? For what? Friedrich doesn't need you. No-one does; and you're the only one who can't see it.

ELIZ: I see what I see: a young woman with no values at all apart from her own vanity, which my brother does no favours by flattering!

LOU: He never flatters me: I wouldn't let him.

ELIZ: No? What would you let him do, then? Not that it's any of my business, of course; but I do feel there are things you ought to know if you're thinking of letting this.. dalliance with my brother turn into something more serious.

LOU: It couldn't be more serious than it is. I love him; in a way someone like you could never understand.

ELIZ: Well, I've never been in love, I freely confess it.

LOU: You surprise me, Frau Nietzsche.

ELIZ: But I do know that lovers ---

LOU: We're not lovers!

ELIZ: Yet - but should that change ---

LOU: It won't.

ELIZ: Really? I'm not sure that's what Friedrich believes. But anyway, as I say: should that change; should you and my brother... well, should you marry, then a husband and wife have conjugal duties --

LOU: Love is not a duty, it's a pleasure, Frau Nietzsche.

ELIZ: And pleasure is so often followed by pain! It won't have escaped you that my brother's health is fragile in the extreme, Fräulein; there are reasons for this ---

LOU: I know ---

ELIZ: Quite specific reasons! - which he may not, almost certainly will not have mentioned to you. And believe me, I mention the subject at all only out of consideration for the health of all those who come into contact with Fritz.

LOU: What are you saying?

ELIZ: Friedrich... my brother has suffered from extreme headaches and increasing neuralgia since his college days...

LOU: And has born it with great stoicism.

ELIZ: Nevertheless, some responsibility must lie in his hands.

LOU: What has this to do with me?

ELIZ: Must I spell it out? *(Beat)* Young men are reckless, they consort with certain types of people, women; live a life they come to regret. My brother's illness dates from that time. It is an illness ---

LOU: It's not an illness!

ELIZ: - An illness which proceeds at its own pace – and for which Mercury is, at best, an emetic palliative.... *(Beat)* Forgive me for trespassing on such delicate ground. Whatever you may think of our relationship, I do so only out of love for my brother - and a concern for those I know he loves, whether I approve of them or not. *(Pause)* I see the information has shocked you, Fräulein; I assure you it was not my intention; but I understand –

LOU: You understand nothing. - Please leave.

ELIZ: *(beat)* I will take my leave from my brother later.

LOU: As you see fit, Frau Nietzsche. Nothing you do or say has any bearing on me. Good day. We won't meet again. *(Beat)*

ELIZ: No, *(acidly)* I trust not.

Lou turns away from Elizabeth. Lights fade to two spots on the women's faces, then fade to black.

2.10

The drawing-room. Next day. Heinrich sits gazing into the fire. Enter Nietzsche, blithely carrying the revolver, which he places on the table.

NIETZ: Look: Santa Claus has come - and only thirty years too late!

HEIN: What?

NIETZ: The gun I always wanted as a child - to shoot my mother with!

HEIN: Then it's a good job you never had one.

NIETZ: Oh I don't know: eight's the age of moral responsibility for a good catholic child; I could've shot her at seven and been all right. *(Inspects the revolver)* Handsome weapon! Found it just past our gate - by the river – swaddled like a baby ---

HEIN: It's mine – *was* mine.

NIETZ: Yours? You secretive old thing, Heinrich. What're you doing with a – *(inspects it)* Gasser 1870?

HEIN: Nothing. Lou was s'posed to get rid of it. It was an experiment.

NIETZ: What in?

HEIN: The opposite of philosophy. You talked about suicide, said you didn't have the money for a gun ---

NIETZ: So you bought me one – how kind!

HEIN: *(deliberate)* I wanted to see what it felt like...

NIETZ: *(hands him back the gun)* Well, now you've got it, shame to waste it: – I'll pretend to make a run for it ---

HEIN: *(sharply)* I'm leaving today. Friedrich. *(Beat)*

NIETZ: Why? I mean, I know why; but you don't have to. *(Beat)* I'm no rival, Heinrich. I know you think I am, but I have no designs... Lou is your... she loves you and ---

HEIN: She loves you too! *(Beat)* As you said: two minds can fall in love....You're a distraction.

NIETZ: Well, I've been called several things in my life ---

HEIN: It's not a joke!

Pause.

As long as she's *here*; as long as *you're* here... she won't be mine.

NIETZ: 'Mine'? 'Yours, his, hers' - we're not possessions, Heinrich, we don't own each other.

HEIN: Yes, we do...! Love *is* possession: two people: 'having and holding'; 'to the exclusion of all others!'

NIETZ: *(Coolly)* Heinrich, be very careful before you bring the bible into this: I *was* the son of a priest, after all.

HEIN: And doesn't it show! Has it ever occurred to you that you owe your whole philosophy to your father? A small-minded, provincial bully who beat you. Every book you've written: one long drawn-out rebellion turned into literature, made into a whole way of life!

(Beat)

NIETZ: *(Again, coolly)* I didn't hate my father... I pitied him.

HEIN: I thought you said pity was a weak emotion!

NIETZ: I never said I haven't been weak. *(Beat)* But I have thought about my weakness. Over time, I mean.

HEIN: Oh, of course you have. You *think* about everything!

NIETZ: - And changed my mind about certain things. You *do know* what that means? To have a change of heart?

HEIN: You can't change yourself just by thinking!

NIETZ: Of course you can! Have you *read any* of my words? Thought *is* action! It changes you, if it hits you here! *(striking his heart)* If you act on it, as I do. *(Suddenly cold)* What do you think thought is, Heinrich – if you'll pardon the pun of course! Well?

HEIN: I think ---

NIETZ: *(Sarcastically)* - 'Therefore I am'? Please! Not dear old Descartes! Rationalist rubbish! So if your heart is broken, doesn't that prove you exist? Shame on you, Heinrich: you're supposed to be the great defender of feelings!

HEIN: I won't argue with you, Friedrich. - Because I don't *want* to win – not that I could, of course, it's your terrain – language, words.

NIETZ: Terrain? Good word. In the context of this .... discussion, I mean. You're right: words do have their own landscape; their own geology even, which we share… whether we like it or not. Tell me, how do you see 'Friendship'? – as a word, I mean.

HEIN: Friedrich ---

NIETZ: What's the feeling of it? Is it a valley? A meadow… what does it conjure up? How does it make you feel, Heinrich?

HEIN: It doesn't make me *'feel'* anything; it's neutral.

NIETZ: *(Barely contained contempt)* No word is neutral; especially the word 'neutral'! In fact 'neutral's the least neutral word in the world. It makes me dead… shut in. Friendship, on the other hand: now that's a landscape. One can go anywhere in it. As long as one is ready for certain rocks, crags, difficult ledges. As I say, words have their own geology. Some are hundreds of thousands of years old… like 'betrayal'…

HEIN: I don't know what you're talking about.

NIETZ: Then there's the bible! - since you mentioned it… 'In the beginning was The Word, and The Word was with God. And The Word *was* God….' That always struck me as strange. I mean, why did God start things with The Word? Why not 'The Fire'? or 'The Storm'? Why something as ordinary as a 'word'? *(Beat)* Except that it isn't ordinary: language is how we take possession of our world…. *(pointedly at Heinrich)* a child is barely human until it begins to speak.

HEIN: Look, I didn't come here for a lecture ---

NIETZ: No, I'm sure you didn't… *(Pause as he calms down)* Actually, I didn't speak proper sentences myself until I was four. My father thought I was backward - or a born atheist. I prefer to think I was thinking *(laughs)* about this strange new life as a parson's son…. But then, can one actually think without words?

HEIN: In dreams.

NIETZ: *(distracted)* What?

HEIN: We don't always think when we dream.

NIETZ: But our dreams make no sense until we do! Precisely! Thought is a frame we place round images. Like paintings. Life is too quick. Thought captures it so we can study it. Meditate upon it – become it, as Lou says!

HEIN: *(Irritated)* What does she say?

NIETZ: - That she becomes the things she writes about. She's right. Look, you and I have no fight. I abhor the use of reason in a cold, clinical way; but the other extreme is no better: romantics are fools!

HEIN: Which, of course, is what I am!

NIETZ: You're worth more, Heinrich!

HEIN: Than what? Love? I'll settle for it! I'll settle for Lou. You can have your philosophy, your 'thought' – take it, you're welcome to it, if it doesn't drive you mad.

NIETZ: Ah yes, the man of action speech. Do you even *know* what an action *is*? How long did it take to fall in love with Lou? A glance? A few words at a party? A dance? Or all the years leading up to your first meeting? Who you *are* is your fate. If I use thought, it's because it sheds a little light, a few shadows on the wall. *(Beat)* God knows, we might as well be in Plato's bloody cave. *(Picks up the revolver again)* You bought this as an experiment: believe me, occasionally death looks like a most attractive escape route.

HEIN: But you never take it.

NIETZ: *(Looks at the revolver)* I prefer a grander exit. Anyway, as I say, actions form a chain. Sometimes I think my whole life has been one slow suicide attempt.

(Pause)

Don't leave. Stay here with Lou. If only to teach me.

HEIN: What can I teach you that you won't disprove in a instant?

(Pause)

NIETZ: How to let go…

Slow fade.

2.9

Nietzsche's study. Next day.

NIETZ: Done! The finest thing I ever wrote!

REE: Though you say so yourself. May one ask what it is?

NIETZ: My resignation letter, of course – to the college!

REE: What! Why?

NIETZ: Ah you thought I was joking about giving up philosophy. Well here's the proof! I have no intention of returning – ever! It's only honest to surrender my salary.

REE: Don't be ridiculous, Friedrich: how will you live?

NIETZ: You'll lend me money of course! *(Beat)* Seriously. I don't know. I haven't a clue – maybe my books will start to sell; if they don't, well, farming!

REE: Farming.

NIETZ: All right: wine-making.

REE: You don't drink.

NIETZ: I'll start.

REE: With *your* health??

NIETZ: All right, I'll work in a shop. Haberdashers! I love all those materials, colours! Warm too: all that sunlight through the windows.

REE: Yes, you're so good with sunlight.

NIETZ: Mmm - true. Then I'll work in a backroom somewhere, do the accounts; I'm good at adding up.

REE: You hate mathematics.

NIETZ: Yes…stop putting obstacles in my way! I'm leaving. I've had enough. Literature! What kind of living is that? One thing Plato *was* right about: writing achieves nothing. All it does is confuse people. I wish I'd been born in some pre-literate age! Direct communication! Man to man! From now on, whatever I have to say, I'll say to men's faces or not at all. To hell with books.

REE: And where will you say it? I mean, this new found zeal for communicating face-to-face with men: where will you practise it? In those marketplaces you love so much?

NIETZ: Yes! No! I don't know: anywhere that gets me out of my bloody room!

REE: I see. *(Beat)* Well – I can only say that I, for one, will miss your books intensely.

NIETZ: Don't say that.

REE: Why not? It's true.

NIETZ: I'm not interested in truth, not this morning anyway.

REE: No, apparently not.

NIETZ: I had a horrible argument with Heinrich. They can't leave! I tried to convince him. He thinks… his idea of love is…it's *not* an idea, it's an addiction: he's addicted to her like a drug; desire is a drug, the more he has the more he wants. He talks about consummation but he can't see he'll never get it.

REE: And you will?

NIETZ: Paul, I want … I *need* a complete change. I can't carry on as I am. I'm sick of writing, thinking… sick of… sick of myself.

REE: Maybe it's not writing that's driving you mad. Maybe it's the kind of writing you do. *(Beat)* Let me turn your own anecdote against you: Socrates on his deathbed? Maybe *you* should just write poetry, music. Before it's too late. *(Pause)* It'll be a great loss of course - to our degenerate world of palsied old philosophers, I mean. But we'll survive. Of course, I blame Lou for all this, for your resignation – revelation, I should call it. Should've seen it a mile off.

NIETZ: Seen what?

REE: Poetry's what happens when philosophy collides with love.

(Pause)

NIETZ: I proposed to her, you know. At least I think I did.

REE: Best to be sure…

NIETZ: Only as a means of protecting her! She and Heinrich are lovers – well, we knew that. What I mean is I merely wished to provide some sort of official basis ---

REE: You really thought Heinrich would accept that?

NIETZ: No. That is, I thought…

REE: And even if he did, do you really think *you* would be satisfied with such an arrangement?

NIETZ: Why not? As I say, they're lovers: I have no desire ---

REE: Really. *(Beat)*

NIETZ: She's a young woman ---

REE: And you're a man – as well as a philosopher.

NIETZ: Twice her age!

REE: - With twice her knowledge of human nature; and its capacity for self-deception...

NIETZ: I love her as *you* love her.

REE: Really? And how do I love her?

NIETZ: What?

REE: Well surely I have a right to know? After all, you seem to know how *I* love her more than you know how *you* love her *yourself*!

NIETZ: Don't be ridiculous!

REE: Look in the mirror before you accuse *me* of that. This whole thing is typical, if I may say so! Typical of you and your attitude to everyone around you! Have you ever stopped to think how I feel about all this? Have you ever asked me once?

NIETZ: About what?

REE: Lou, for Christ's sake!

NIETZ: But I thought ---

REE: Thought what? That I would just go along with anything you wanted; agree with everything you said! As it happens, I do, but that's not the point! *(Beat. Exasperated with himself as well as Nietzsche)* What *is* the point? Look at us. Couple of old fools. I really thought... - what *did* I think?

Pause.

NIETZ: What are we to do? *(Beat)* Lou asked me the same thing the other day: I came up with some trite answer.

REE: There *is* no answer.

NIETZ: No, forgive me, I've been stupid. Love reduces one to such banalities.... *(Beat)* I'm tired ---

He suddenly steadies himself against the chair.

REE: Friedrich? Are you all right? Give me your arm.

NIETZ: No, I'm all right. I need a bit of air, it's stuffy in here; a quick walk'll do it. *(Laughs)* The shock, you see - of being found out…I always said philosophers were frauds.

REE: And idiots.. and dupes and…

NIETZ: Not much of a profession, as I said.

REE: Oh I can think of worse – like a haberdasher, or accountant. Forgive me if I throw away your resignation letter whilst you're asleep.

NIETZ: I'll only write another one.

Exit Nietzsche. Rée takes up said letter, screws it up, then thinks again, unscrews it and begins to read it. Enter Lou looking preoccupied.

LOU : I thought I heard Friedrich.

REE: You've just missed him. You'll catch him if you hurry, he went outside to clear his head…

LOU : No, it's all right. I'll… *(Beat)* We're going, Paul.

REE: Where, down to town, do you want some company…

LOU: No, no – I mean, leaving.

REE: Leaving? Leaving for where?

LOU : We're going back to Munich.

REE: What? – Why? When? - Forgive me, I'm overcome by interrogatives - has everyone gone mad this morning?! First Friedrich comes in throwing around resignation letters, now this!

LOU: I've got to go.

REE: Seriously?

LOU: For Friedrich's sake.

REE: I'm sorry but how can your departure possibly benefit Friedrich? Has he said something? Is it something the silly fool's said? Don't listen to him: he's just a philosopher: we're paid to say stupid things – in a clever way, of course ---

LOU: No, no. I spoke to his sister.

REE: Her! Surely you're not listening to anything that rabid lunatic comes out with? You do know it was a full moon last night: she's at her worst ---

LOU: It's not what she said, which was predictably vile.

REE: What? What *did* she say?

LOU: Nothing.

REE: She must've said something!

LOU: We talked about Fritz's illness, the causes ---

REE: What causes?

LOU: His college days, reckless behaviour, women, stupid stuff..

REE: Reckless behaviour – Fritz? What on earth … Ah now I see: Fritz the great Lothario! How she'd love that moral diagnosis! - If only Fritz did have the clap! Sadly, he's led a blameless life; half his problem in my opinion: lack of worldly experience is a weakness in a philosopher.

LOU: Paul, be serious.

REE: I'm sorry, I can't when it comes to that woman.

LOU: I told you it's not what she said! It's the fact that she's here at all; that she follows him everywhere; that he allows her to! I can't bear being in the same room; I can't even stand thinking about her. *(Beat)* Anyway, it's not just that. *(Beat)* Heinrich isn't happy.

REE: Lovers never are – for long.

LOU: But he says he could be – would be - if I were with him.

REE: You *are* with him ---

LOU: On my own.

REE: I see.

LOU: Everything's got too complicated. It was supposed to be simple: coming here, living like this – together.

REE: I did warn Friedrich.

LOU: About what?

REE: The difference between theory and practice, *(beat)* where love is concerned.

Pause.

LOU: I have a train to catch.

REE: You must see Friedrich - at least tell him.

LOU: How? It's difficult to explain.

REE: You're telling me!

LOU: I'll write.

REE: - What? A poem, a play?

LOU: Paul, you're not helping.

REE: No, I'm not – I'm doing whatever I can to stop you going. It's madness.

LOU: I need some time away - to think.

REE: Time to think? What else have you got here?

LOU: Unhappiness.

REE: Then go and put it right.

She starts to exit then turns back.

LOU: You've always been so kind.

REE: Have I? ...Don't feel kind. Right now I feel I want to lock you in your room until you see sense. *(Beat)* You know I'm not just arguing for Fritz's sake... I always felt.... I think I... what I wanted to say is....

Sees she has looked away.

I'll miss you.

She turns back and looks at him. Fade.

2.11

The garden. The sound of birdsong. Light filtering through the trees. Lou approaches Nietzsche who is sitting on a bench

LOU: I'm sorry, I'm disturbing you ---

NIETZ: You never disturb me – except with the pleasure of seeing you.

LOU: Friedrich, please...

NIETZ: Well, who else likes you as much as I do – apart from those other two rogues, I mean?

LOU: Your sister says you're making my vanity worse.

NIETZ: Impossible.

LOU: Very funny. I keep telling Heinrich I'm not some damned angel..

NIETZ: No, you're vain and conceited and attractive and funny and irritable and – oh I don't know, all the things that make up a beautiful young woman!

LOU: See? Your sister's right.

NIETZ: Not a phrase one enjoys hearing…

She sits down next to him, takes his hand.

LOU: They're delicate – more like a pianist's than a writer's. Another thing your sister's right about…

NIETZ: My sister! My sister is a busy-body who should find herself a proper vocation in life – apart from meddling in other people's affairs – principally mine. And if she knew the first thing about musicians, which she doesn't, she'd know that all the best pianists actually possess rather short, stubby digits. Long slender fingers is an old cliché.

LOU: Still, your hands *are* delicate.

NIETZ: Because they've never done any real work.

LOU: Not true, they've wielded the wisest pen in Europe – the world.

NIETZ: Flattery'll get you everywhere, Lou; don't stop.

LOU: I saw her today; your sister, I mean.

NIETZ: Really? Bad luck. Strange, she didn't come and see me - thank god. What did she have to say?

LOU: She said… we had an argument.

NIETZ: Oh? Serious, I hope? Have you broken off all contact with her?

LOU: Yes.

NIETZ: Excellent. *(Beat)* Lou, are you sure you're all right?

LOU: Yes, I'm well. Are you? I mean, feeling well...

NIETZ: Yes, of course. Why, shouldn't I be? Apart from all the usual reasons!

LOU: Yes. It's just... I think you're very brave.

NIETZ: Really? About what exactly?

LOU: Everything. Life. Your illness.

NIETZ: Oh that: Yes, I lie in bed for days feeling sorry for myself. I've actually got rather good at it over the years ---

LOU: Be serious, Friedrich. Isn't there someone you could see?

NIETZ: See?

LOU: To help you: a doctor, I mean?

Beat. Nietzsche adopts contrived 'serious' face.

NIETZ: Yes, actually there *is* someone now you mention it: he's called Doctor Von Quack from Quack-berg! Lou, are you sure you're all right.

LOU: Yes! - But there must be something they can do...

NIETZ: Why? I mean, yes, I used to hope... not anymore. This thing, attacks - call them what you like: I have to live with them: that's all there is to it.

LOU: Is it? You could change. Do something completely different. So much of your life revolves around things, people, that do you no good.

NIETZ: Not anymore – that's all changed. Since we came here, all the disquiet I used to feel; when I was alone, I mean, without a soul.. something in me has... *you* have quietened something in me. You know what I feel like these days? One of those eternal Tuscan summer

(Nietzsche cont.)

afternoons when the world's asleep. You know: the valley's empty, fields of sunflowers; time itself seems to lay down its tools: it's too hot to do anything – except dream. You've given me a kind of peace. Even when I wake I feel different; I used to feel anxious: as if something were pressing down on me: something I hadn't done, or had to do. But now I... it doesn't seem to matter so much. Even people have stopped annoying me, goddamit. As you said: life is a marketplace, one can't escape men. There, you see: look what you've done to me. Actually, I'm beginning to worry that I might be on the verge of something terrible...

LOU: What?

NIETZ: Being happy. *(Beat)* Then what would I do? I'd have no reason to think, no reason to philosophise – because I'd feel no pain. Pain is a sign of interesting terrain: all the best thoughts come from crossing that border.

LOU: So long as you can rejoin the land of the living.

NIETZ: Yes. Well I *am* in the land of the living – and I want to stay here – for as long as you're here too...

LOU: Yes - It's been lovely...

NIETZ: It still *is* lovely.

LOU: Yes, I never could've believed... it's been ---

NIETZ: Why are you using the past tense?

LOU: I'm not. I'm just saying - you always say the only constant thing is change. *(Beat)* Perhaps we should part, just for a while – to keep all this alive! While we still believe in it.

NIETZ: What? What are you talking about?

LOU: Love doesn't last: you said so yourself.

NIETZ: That doesn't mean we should kill it! Anyway, I wasn't talking about love; I meant romance. Romance doesn't last, can't last: its predicated on conditions which ---

LOU: Heinrich has asked – demanded a decision. He wants me to go with him.

NIETZ: Where?

LOU: Back to Germany – just for a week or two. Then, perhaps travel a little…

NIETZ: I see.

LOU: I know it's sudden. I don't know what to do.

NIETZ: Why must you do anything?

LOU: He'll leave ---

NIETZ: And come back: that's what lovers do.

LOU: What if he doesn't? I do love him, Friedrich; I don't want to lose the chance… I don't want to lose him.

NIETZ: Then go to him.

Pause.

LOU: You don't mind?

NIETZ: Why should I? As long as you come back. I'll still be here. Well, I might be back in Nice, or Portofino. When summer ends, I mean. You shouldn't miss that moment on the Mediterranean - when the tourists are all gone. There's a secret mystery to the place. Promise me you'll come and see it! - Actually you *hear* it first: festivity dies away in the streets, and in the fields the Italian crickets play their music a little quieter each evening, until one night the hillside is completely silent, and you know summer's finally gone - taken all his retinue with him and cleared out completely… and a new guest is here. *(Beat)* There's a beautiful melancholy in the silence of a deserted city, streets

(Nietzsche cont.)

cloistered with shadow: as a northerner one is betrayed every year by the death of summer. Wherever you stay: sunset bereaves the streets, veils them in a kind of grief. One is widowed by thoughts of winter - my own fault! One mourns a naïve dependency upon the sun...

Pause.

But you'll come, we'll meet up there - or wherever we are at the time. Won't you?

LOU   Yes... of course! I'm glad you... I ought to go. Goodbye Friedrich.

NIETZ: Goodbye Lou....

She turns, turns back, turns again, is just about to exit when Nietzsche speaks in a clear almost neutral monotone.

Don't go.

She stops but doesn't turn round.

LOU: I must.

NIETZ: Why?

LOU: I've told you.

NIETZ: You've told me nothing. Yes, yes, Heinrich wants to marry you. I understand that: I predicted it!

LOU: Predicted it?

NIETZ: Hardly difficult: you're both young, passionate, full of enthusiasms.

LOU: A little more than enthusiasm ---

NIETZ: I just thought you'd both be, well, a little less commonplace about it, that's all; spouting trite nonsense about love.

LOU: We're not *spouting* anything!

NIETZ: Platitudes! As if romance wasn't a big enough cliché already! I mean, please don't tell me that you and Von Holstein --

LOU: Heinrich.

NIETZ: Yes, yes Heinrich – that you and he are just going to go salon-hopping round the moronic reception rooms of Hanover? Playing little Mr and Mrs Von-aristocrat!

LOU: Why not? Isn't that what you wanted?

NIETZ: What?

LOU: If I'd said 'yes' to you, your proposal of marriage: wouldn't we have done the same thing? Only with you it would've been fawning over Wagner and his old maid of a wife! Actually, what is it you see in these domineering females, Friedrich? Cosima, your sister, your mother---

NIETZ: Don't be preposterous.

LOU: What is it you really want from *me*, apart from some docile girl sitting at your feet like a lapdog?

NIETZ: For god's sake, if I'd wanted that don't you think I could have had it from a hundred women before now?

LOU: I don't know: could you? Sometimes I think you haven't the slightest clue what you want from women - principally because you're too afraid to find out.

NIETZ: *(quiet, stunned)* How could you say that?

LOU: Don't tell me I've shocked you, Friedrich.

NIETZ: *(now cold)* What I've said about women, I stand by. I've never said I admired your sex as such.

LOU: 'My sex as such' – what is that?

NIETZ: Women in general.

LOU: So I'm 'women in general'!

NIETZ: No!

LOU: What then?

NIETZ: You know that's not what I meant! Look, please let's not turn this into a vile argument.

LOU: Why not? I thought we were supposed to be honest with each other whatever the cost.

NIETZ: Truthful – not brutal!

LOU: *(coldly)* But you like cruelty. Isn't that part of your philosophy? The celebration of force!

NIETZ: No, no. Not between us!

LOU: Liar.

NIETZ: Lou.. please…

LOU: Confront the truth, however bitter things taste! Well here they are!

NIETZ: Please! Stop! *(Beat)* You're distorting everything I've said. This is absurd. I'm sorry if I've said some stupid things… but you provoked me.

LOU: *I* provoked *you*?

NIETZ: Deliberately aimed to hurt *(beat)* – women are born assassins: I'm only sorry I presented such an obvious target.

LOU: Oh don't apologise Friedrich; you are only human, after all. Your book titles say it all. Perhaps you should read what you've written occasionally.

NIETZ: What's that supposed to mean?

LOU: That you're a man, Friedrich – sometimes you behave with less than angelic qualities yourself!

NIETZ: And you, fräulein, behave like a typical woman!

LOU: Really, well a bit of news for you, Friedrich: I *am* a woman.

NIETZ: That's no reason to behave like one. You lured me here – let me set this whole thing up. Even my stupid sister could see it: you're not serious about anything; no better than a coquette, flirting with everything: philosophy, art, men! – For what? So you can flatter yourself with your own reflection. God knows, women never do anything without a mirror to hand. More fool me! Evidently the brilliant young woman I proposed to was a trick of the light - a trick of some kind, anyway. Well, trust me I won't fall for it twice.

LOU: No - well I wouldn't give you the pleasure! Not that you'd know what to do with pleasure anyway - whatever your dear sister has to say on the matter!

NIETZ: Oh please don't bring her into it!

LOU: No, well, no need to: she's here already, isn't she? Looking over our shoulders, inspecting your behaviour, spying on your every move!

NIETZ: What are you talking about?

He begins to approach her.

LOU: *(Mockingly)* Your sister, Friedrich: the only woman who understands you! The only woman you can bear to let near you!

NIETZ: How dare you. You ---

He takes hold of her, pause, suddenly he tries to kiss her, she lets him coldly, then flinches, then wrestles free.

Lou --- !

She begins to exit but is cut off by the entrance of Heinrich.

HEIN: I'm sorry, I thought I heard raised voices.

LOU: – I want to go! - Now!

NIETZ: Look - Lou...

HEIN: What's happened?

LOU: Nothing. That's the problem, isn't it, Friedrich? Nothing ever happens between you and .... *(Silence, then very cool)* Apparently I'm a disappointment. - Oh yes, and you and I are couple of walking clichés! What was it...

NIETZ: Please... I'm sorry ---

LOU: Well perhaps we'd better not disappoint him.

NIETZ: Forgive me: I've been unpardonable. I just couldn't bear ---

HEIN: Couldn't bear what, Friedrich: the thought of losing someone you love?

LOU: Heinrich I want to go ---

NIETZ: Yes! *(beat)* - that we *all* love.

HEIN: And the rest of it, Friedrich? All the theories, accepting everything! '*Rising* above ourselves'...?

NIETZ: We should, but...

HEIN: But what?

NIETZ: There must be some basic principle...

HEIN: Principle..?

NIETZ: Of friendship, love; you're the ones leaving, for god's sake!

LOU: Heinrich, please: are you coming?

NIETZ: Why? *(Beat)* Tell me: I have a right to some explanation!

HEIN: It's run its course, can't you see? It doesn't work.

NIETZ: It does! It has worked! Tell him, Lou.

Heavy pause.

LOU: Friedrich... I love you.

HEIN: What?

LOU: And so does Heinrich. But we're leaving. People aren't works of art, Friedrich. They're flawed, they can't be made perfect. Paradise doesn't exist, you said so yourself.

She turns and leaves. Heinrich exchanges glances with Nietzsche and exits on:

HEIN: Lou..!

As Nietzsche is left standing, lights fade.

2.12

Nietzsche's room. Morning. Weeks later. Sunlight splits through a chink in the curtains. Nietzsche is asleep on his chaise. Enter Rée.

REE: Friedrich..? I'll be on my way. - Oh I'm sorry.

NIETZ: No, no, come in. I've been asleep far too long. Couple of years, judging by my head...

Rée picks up a bottle of Laudanum.

REE: This won't have helped. *(Beat)*

NIETZ: I couldn't get to sleep for hours – now I can't wake up… not that I planned to - thought I'd taken enough to sink a battleship.

REE: I trust you're joking.

NIETZ: I'll be fine… *(gives him a wry glance.)*

REE: You're sure?

NIETZ: Of course! I'm Prussian, aren't I! *(Affects a wry, unsteady half salute, then holds his head)* God. My head.

Pause.

REE: What will you do?

NIETZ: I don't know. *(Beat)* Where are you staying in Paris?

REE: George's. Just for a week or two; then I thought perhaps London. Why don't you come?

NIETZ: No thanks, I can't stand tea. I think I'll stay here a little longer.

Pause.

So quiet in here.

REE: Too quiet. Come to Paris.

NIETZ: I would - but you might introduce me to another scintillating young woman, then where would we be?

Pause

REE: It was good while it lasted, Fritz.

NIETZ: Yes. The past tense is such a bore – full of ghosts…. Have you heard? – anything about them, I mean.

REE: Here and there. Last letter I got they were back in St Petersburg; Lou has broken with her mother ---

NIETZ: Again.

REE: Again.

NIETZ: And dear Heinrich?

REE: He's busy making plans for their winter retreat across Russia! - Sent his love by the way.

NIETZ: Return it. *(Pause)* I said some vile things.

REE: Heat of the moment..

NIETZ: Burnt into memory forever. If I could take them back...

Pause.

REE: So what *will* you do?

NIETZ: What I always do: get up, have breakfast, stare into the middle distance; god knows, might even write a few lists! *(Beat)* Lou didn't answer my last letter. Maybe she didn't get it! Do you think it would make any difference if I wrote to them again jointly...? *(Beat)* No, nor do I... - So! Paris! City of light!

REE: City of light.

They embrace.

REE: I'll write – a day or two after I get there.

NIETZ: Go - while the going's good.

REE: You're sure you'll be all right?

NIETZ: *(Wry)* No. I'll be miserable as sin. So miserable, in fact, that I may have to write a book about it. Week or two of poetic despair! What could be better!

They embrace again. Rée leaves. A Pause then Nietzsche goes over to the window, opens it and calls out to Rée.

(Nietzsche cont.)

Send my regards to the land of the living..!

Nietzsche peers out to see Rée depart, waves, then winces at the sunlight. He then starts to close the curtains, but pauses for a second, and slowly, evenly draws the curtains apart again, to stand drenched, almost crucified by sunlight. He lets his arms slowly drop to his sides. Slow fade to black on his silhouette at the window.

End

To Hell in a Handcart

© 2018 by James Murphy.

All rights reserved.

Published by The Heretic's Press
London
www.hereticspress.co.uk

By the same author

Poets (play-script)
The art of Exile (poetry)
The Misanthropist's Secret Love Life (poetry)
Lyrical Cynicism (poetry)
Disposophobia (play-script)
Crash the Bus (novel)
Handbook for the Damned (cultural & literary criticism)

ISBN 978-1-9996149-2-8
© 2018 The Heretic's Press
www.hereticspress.co.uk